SHAREPOINT FLOWS

FROM SCRATCH

PETER KALMSTRÖM

SHAREPOINT FLOWS FROM SCRATCH

Welcome to *SharePoint Flows from Scratch*! This book gives the basic knowledge needed to automate SharePoint business processes with the Microsoft Flow service.

SharePoint Flows from Scratch is intended for SharePoint Online administrators, content creators and other power users who already know their way around SharePoint. (If you are new to SharePoint, you will probably find my book *SharePoint Online from Scratch* more useful, *refer to* https://www.kalmstrom.com/Education/SharePoint-Online.htm.)

In my work as a SharePoint consultant, I have come to understand what automation areas are the most important to SharePoint power users, and the book focuses on those areas.

The questions I get are most often concrete – "How do I...?, or "Can a flow...?" – and I hope this book will give the answers to the most common of them. Therefore, *SharePoint Flows from Scratch* has many images and step by step instructions.

To be even clearer, I often refer to my online video demonstrations. These videos have been recorded during more than a year, and in that time Microsoft has made changes to the SharePoint and Flow interfaces. Therefore, some demos might show an interface that is not the latest one. Don't mind that, the flow will still work in the same way. Even in this book you may discover things that have changed since the book was published, but I am sure you will understand it anyway.

Microsoft Flow is intended for use with cloud applications and services, and in this book I focus on flows where SharePoint Online is included and plays an important role.

Flow has a "no code" approach, but if you have some development knowledge you can do more with the service. However, even if you don't know much about coding, you can use the code blocks offered in Flow, and some such blocks are included and explained in this book.

SharePoint Flows from Scratch has two parts. After several chapters with general information, I give examples on how flows can be used to automate common business processes. I recommend that you actually create these example flows yourself and not just read about them. That way you will learn to manage Flow, and you will discover a lot more about the service than I have included in this book.

Good luck with your studies!

Peter Kalmström

TABLE OF CONTENTS

INTRODUCTION 8

1   WHY AUTOMATE? 9
   1.1   Accuracy..9
   1.2   Tracking..9
   1.3   Speed..9
2   IMPORTANT TO CONSIDER...10
   2.1   Storage...10
   2.2   Changes in SharePoint 10
   2.3   CamelCase Naming 11
3   FLOW PLANS...13
   3.1   Environments 13
   3.2   Premium Connectors 13
4   THE FLOW ADMIN CENTER 14
   4.1   Data Policies...15
5   IMPORTANT CONCEPTS 17
   5.1   Connectors 17
      5.1.1   From Template...19
      5.1.2   From Blank..19
      5.1.3   Approvals 20
         5.1.3.1   Request sign-off 20
      5.1.4   Schedule...21
      5.1.5   Variables 21
      5.1.6   Button 23
   5.2   Trigger..23
      5.2.1   Template Trigger.....................................23
      5.2.2   From Blank Trigger 23
      5.2.3   Recurrence..25
   5.3   Actions..26
      5.3.1   Conditions..28
      5.3.2   Apply to Each 29
      5.3.3   Delay a flow 30
      5.3.4   E-mail Actions 30
   5.4   Hard-coded Text..30
   5.5   Dynamic Content..31
   5.6   Expressions...32
      5.6.1   Add the expression to the flow 33
6   START CREATING A FLOW 34
   6.1   The Flow Site 34
      6.1.1   Reach the Flow Site.................................35
         6.1.1.1   From SharePoint Online 35
   6.2   Start from a Template...36

6.3		*Start from Blank*	*38*
	6.3.1	Choose Connector and Trigger	38
6.4		*Start from an Existing Flow*	*40*
6.5		*Build the Flow*	*41*
	6.5.1	Renaming	43
6.6		*New Step*	*43*
6.7		*Create your First Flow – Send Skype Message on New Task*	*44*
	6.7.1	Prerequisites	45
	6.7.2	Theory	45
	6.7.3	Steps	45
	6.7.4	Test the flow	47
6.8		*Finalize the Flow*	*48*
	6.8.1	Test	48
	6.8.1.1	Schedule flows	49
	6.8.1.2	Difficult triggers	49
	6.8.2	Edit a Flow	49
	6.8.3	Troubleshoot a Flow	50
	6.8.3.1	Errors while Building	50
	6.8.4	Errors while Testing	51
	6.8.5	Errors while in Production	53
7		SHARE A FLOW	55
7.1		*Team Flows*	*55*
7.2		*Export and Import Flows*	*57*
	7.2.1	Export a flow	57
	7.2.2	Import a flow	58
	7.2.2.1	Update an existing flow	58
	7.2.2.2	Create a new flow	59
EXAMPLE FLOWS			**61**
8		SET DOCUMENT TITLES	62
8.1		*Theory*	*62*
	8.1.1	SharePoint	62
	8.1.2	Flow	63
8.2		*Flow for Existing Libraries*	*63*
	8.2.1	Prerequisites	63
	8.2.2	Steps	63
	8.2.3	Update Existing Files	64
8.3		*Flow for New Documents*	*65*
	8.3.1	Prerequisites	65
	8.3.2	Steps	65
9		APPROVAL FLOWS	66
9.1		*Approval with the Built-in 'Approval Status' Column*	*66*
	9.1.1	Prerequisites	67
	9.1.2	Theory	67
	9.1.2.1	SharePoint, built-in approval status column	67
	9.1.2.2	Flow	68
	9.1.3	Steps	68

9.2   Approval with a Custom Approval Status Column *70*
   9.2.1   Prerequisites 70
   9.2.2   Theory 70
      9.2.2.1   SharePoint, custom column for approval status 70
   9.2.3   Steps 71
9.3   Approval Flow in a Mobile *72*
10   GET E-MAIL INPUT ON NEW ITEMS 74
  10.1   Prerequisites *74*
  10.2   Theory *74*
  10.3   Steps *75*
11   CALCULATE TOTALS 77
  11.1   Prerequisites: *78*
  11.2   Theory *78*
   11.2.1   SharePoint 78
   11.2.2   Flow 78
  11.3   Steps *78*
12   PROGRESS BAR 80
  12.1   Prerequisites: *80*
  12.2   Theory *80*
   12.2.1   SharePoint 81
   12.2.2   Flow 81
  12.3   Steps *81*
13   MONTHLY PROJECTS REPORT 83
  13.1   Prerequisites *83*
  13.2   Theory *83*
  13.3   Steps *84*
14   FORMAT E-MAIL BODY 87
  14.1   Prerequisites: *87*
  14.2   Theory *88*
  14.3   Steps *88*
15   E-MAIL LINKS 90
16   ROLL BACK COLUMN CHANGES 92
  16.1   Prerequisites *92*
  16.2   Theory *92*
  16.3   Steps *92*
17   SET TASK ASSIGNEE DEPENDING ON CATEGORY 95
  17.1   Prerequisites: *95*
  17.2   Theory *96*
  17.3   Steps *96*
18   MERGE ORDERS INTO A TASKS LIST 98
  18.1   Prerequisites *98*
  18.2   Theory *99*
   18.2.1   SharePoint 99
   18.2.2   Flow 99
  18.3   Steps *99*

19   COPY SURVEY RESPONSES FROM FORMS 102
   19.1   Prerequisites: 102
   19.2   Theory 102
   19.3   Steps 103
20   COPY REQUESTED DROPBOX FILES TO SHAREPOINT..................................... 106
   20.1   Prerequisites 106
   20.2   Theory 107
   20.3   Steps 107
21   NEW EMPLOYEE TASKS 109
   21.1   New Employee Tasks without a Settings List 109
       21.1.1   Prerequisites 109
       21.1.2   Theory 109
       21.1.3   Steps 110
   21.2   New Employee Tasks with a Settings List 111
       21.2.1   Prerequisites 111
       21.2.2   Theory 112
       21.2.3   Steps 112
22   KEEP TWO LISTS IN SYNC 114
   22.1   Prerequisites 114
   22.2   Set Manager for New Employees.. 114
       22.2.1   Theory 114
       22.2.2   Steps 114
   22.3   Update Employees List With Manager Changes........................... 116
       22.3.1   Theory 116
       22.3.2   Steps 116
23   REMINDERS 118
   23.1   Event Reminder... 118
       23.1.1   Prerequisites 118
       23.1.2   Theory 118
       23.1.3   Steps 118
   23.2   Contract Review Reminder 120
       23.2.1   Prerequisites 120
       23.2.2   Theory 121
       23.2.3   Steps 121
24   SEND E-MAILS WITH ATTACHMENTS FROM SHARED MAILBOX 124
   24.1   Prerequisites 124
   24.2   Theory 124
   24.3   Steps 124

ABOUT THE AUTHOR..128

INDEX...129

INTRODUCTION

At the beginning of 2016, Microsoft introduced a new service for workflow creation in addition to the traditional SharePoint workflows: Microsoft Flow. Workflows created with Flow are sometimes called "workflows" and sometimes "flows", but in this book I will call the Flow creations "flows", to separate them from the workflows created in SharePoint Designer and the built-in SharePoint workflows.

Flow can integrate across multiple data sources and deliver across multiple devices, from desktop to mobile. The flows can be used extensively for many cloud based services, and often several of these services are combined in one flow. If you, for example, want to copy all new files in a Dropbox folder to a folder in a SharePoint Online document library, you need to use a flow.

Flow is primarily intended for Office 365 and other cloud based platforms, but with a data gateway and a paid plan you can connect to Flow to on-premises data sources. And even if you use SharePoint on-premises, you can of course take advantage of Flow to administer other cloud services. (Most organizations will have some resources on-premises and some in the cloud for the foreseeable future).

In this book, I will focus on flows that are created with SharePoint Online as one of the included services. SharePoint flows can be used in all kinds of SharePoint Online lists and libraries to automate time consuming or repetitive processes.

SharePoint flows are often used for notification sending, but they can also calculate time, archive list items, update apps and perform many other tasks that would have been tedious – or not performed at all – if they were not automated.

Microsoft wants Flow to be a no-code, rapid application development environment, and as such it has certain limitations. However, given that you have a possibility to call a REST service from a flow, the Flow potential is almost limitless. (A REST service is a common standard for communicating with services from many vendors).

Flows are built online, at https://flow.microsoft.com, in the Flow Editor. You create the flow step by step in boxes whose content varies with each flow. There is also a mobile app, and I use it in one of the example flows.

When you create a flow, you can either start with a blank flow or use a template that you modify so that it suits your system and requirements.

1   WHY AUTOMATE?

Before we start looking into Microsoft Flow and how to create flows, I will point out why you should automate business processes in the first place. As you are reading this book, you probably already know why, but maybe you will still find it useful to have my opinion on the benefits of SharePoint automation compared to manual processes.

1.1   ACCURACY

Most organizations have processes that need to be performed in a specific way and order, and the best way to make sure this is done is to automate them. When processes are performed manually, you can never be sure that everything is done 100% correctly.

People make mistakes. Even if you check and double-check your work there will be errors, and these are often difficult to find. People also get bored and are prone to do variations, which might lead to further mistakes.

A flow, on the other hand, always works in the same way. Once you have tested the flow and made sure that it works as it should, you can rely on its accuracy.

1.2   TRACKING

With a flow, it is easy to track processes. Flows can log and document what has been done, something that is often requested by the management and sometimes even by law. Such tasks are often tedious and boring to perform manually, and tend to be performed insufficiently or not at all.

When you let flows keep track of what happens, you will also have documentation. A flow can for example add items in a SharePoint list or comments in a list column, describing what has been done and why.

1.3   SPEED

It takes time to build a flow, but the flow creation time will be well spent if you have a process that must be performed repeatedly. Once the flow is tested and works well, no more time has to be spent on the process, but to do it manually takes time over and over again.

Furthermore, the flow in itself is quicker than a human. Even if flows normally have a delay of 5 minutes, they perform most processes much quicker than a human can do.

Demo: https://www.kalmstrom.com/Tips/SharePoint-Flows/Flow-Why-Automate.htm

2   IMPORTANT TO CONSIDER

I hope you want to try a lot of flows and that you will enjoy experimenting with the service. However, before you start using Flow in production, there are some things you must be aware of.

2.1   STORAGE

Flows are stored in the personal account of the user who created them (and in the region that hosts the environment of that user, if multiple environments are used). This might be good for personal flows and experimenting, but it creates issues if a user who has created flows for the organization leaves his/her position.

Therefore, any organization that decides to automate things with flows, should make sure that flows are not limited to one person's user account. Instead, the organization must be able to continue using and editing the flow even if a user leaves the organization, and also manage potential costs in cases of high volume flows.

There are two solutions:

- Dedicated account. Create a special user account that is used for all flows that automate business processes within the organization. I would recommend giving it a full E3 license, so that you can send e-mails from flows, access SharePoint and so on.

  Flow generated e-mails by default have the flow creator as sender, so a dedicated account will also give a better sender address.

  A drawback with this solution is that the number of flow runs allowed each month is counted per user, not per tenant, so if the organization uses many flows that run often, the next solution might be better.

- Team flows. If all flows that manage processes in the organization are shared, there are multiple owners to each flow. This can work very well as long as you make sure that all flows used in production really are shared. *Refer to* chapter 7, Share a Flow.

2.2   CHANGES IN SHAREPOINT

If you are used to SharePoint workflows, you know that the workflow continues to run even if you change the name of a list or a column that is used in the workflow.

In Flow it is more complicated, because when you change a list or column name that is included in a flow, you have to change the name in the flow also. Otherwise the flow will stop working.

The more mission-critical your flows are, the more serious this issue becomes. You might want to consider taking away the default permission for users to modify column names by not giving them

Contribute permissions on the SharePoint site or list instead of the default Edit permission.

2.3 CAMELCASE NAMING

CamelCase naming is when you write two separate words together without a space and use capital first letters in both words. *SharePoint* is a good example.

I have noticed that flows work best if you use CamelCase naming for SharePoint apps and columns. This will give an URL without the irritating "%20" that is automatically placed instead of a space, because the internal SharePoint name has no spaces.

Below the internal name is written in CamelCase, "SalesLibrary", but in the user interface the name is the more readable "Sales Library".

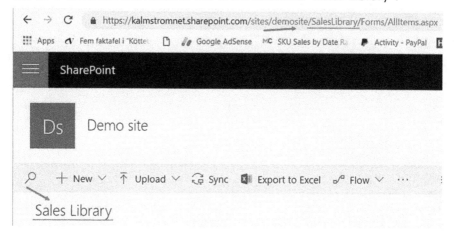

Do like this to have internal CamelCase names and other names that are visible to users:

1. Create an app or a column and write the name in CamelCase style.

2. Save the app/column.

3. Open the app/column settings and change the name into something that is more suitable for users.

4. Now the CamelCase name will be the internal name, that you can see in the URL. In the user interface, the second name will be visible instead.

I have used this method when creating the example flows in this book, but when I mention names of apps and columns I most often choose the more readable name with a space.

As I am human and do both mistakes and variations I am not always consistent in this, but I do recommend being as consistent as possible.

Demo:
https://www.kalmstrom.com/Tips/SharePoint-Online-Course/CamelCase-Naming.htm

3 FLOW PLANS

Flow is included in the Office 365 Enterprise and Business Premium and Essentials subscriptions. However, the Flow features included in the standard subscription can be enhanced with Plan1 and Plan2 subscriptions.

I will not go into the Plan enhancements here, because I think my readers first want to try the regular services before they start thinking about enhancements. All images below are taken from a standard Enterprise subscription with no extra Plan added.

However, some features that are only available in the Plans are visible on the Flow site (where flows are created, *see* below) even if they are not included in the standard services and no additional subscription has been paid for. It is even possible to start – deliberate or accidental – trials of these Plans from within Flow when you try to use features that are only included in the Plans.

Note: A short time before this book was published, Microsoft announced that some current standard features would not be free for Office 365 users in the future. What affects this book seems to be the possibility to add links in e-mails. This feature will require a Plan after 1 February 2019 or when the current Office 365 subscription expires.

You can find the details on the plans at https://flow.microsoft.com/pricing/.

3.1 ENVIRONMENTS

An environment is a space to store your organization's flows, powerapps, and business data. You can use environments to separate flows that have different roles, security requirements or targets.

A single environment is automatically created for each tenant and shared by all users in that tenant. By default all users can create flows in that environment.

With the Plan 2 enhancement, tenant administrators can create more environments in the Flow Admin center. Using environments gives a performance benefit, but it also means that the flow is limited to the resources of that environment.

3.2 PREMIUM CONNECTORS

Flow lets you connect to a wide range of online services. The Plans include even more services, called Premium connectors. In some views they are visible even though you cannot connect to them, and when you try, you are prompted to upgrade to a Plan. Also *refer to* 5.1, Connectors.

4 THE FLOW ADMIN CENTER

You can find a link to the Flow Admin center in the Office 365 Admin center. Note that the Flow and PowerApps admin centers are connected, so any changes you make in the Flow Admin center will impact the PowerApps Admin center and vice versa. Therefore, these two can actually be considered as one Admin center for both services.

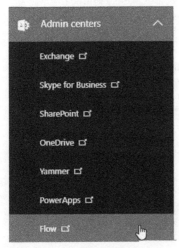

When you click on 'Flow' under 'Admin centers', you will be directed to https://admin.flow.microsoft.com.

Without any Plan addition, you cannot do much in this Admin center, but there are still some valuable features. You can download a CSV file with data about user licenses, and you can also see how much of your Flow quota you have used. (The Office 365 subscription gives 2000 runs per month and user account, which is enough for most organizations. To have more, you must subscribe to a Plan.)

You can also set Data policies for the tenant in the Flow/PowerApps Admin center.

4.1 DATA POLICIES

To prevent business data from being published to external services, such as social media sites, tenant admins can set Data Retention Policies in the Flow/PowerApps Admin center. Select 'Data Policies' in the left pane and click on 'New policy' in the top right corner.

There is a selection which environments the new policy should be applied to, but without an extra Plan you only have one environment and can only choose the first option, 'Apply to ALL environments'.

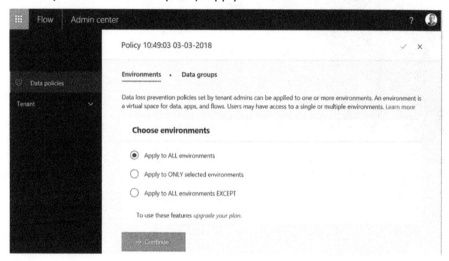

When you click on 'Continue', the 'Data groups' tab will open. Here you will see all available services and how they are grouped in 'Business data only' and 'No business data allowed'.

Data sources that contain business critical data, such as SharePoint and SQL, should go into the 'Business data only' group, while those that do not contain protected information would go to the 'No business data allowed' group. When you add a service to one of the data groups, it will automatically be removed from the other group.

When users create a powerapp or a flow, they are not allowed to combine connections from both groups.

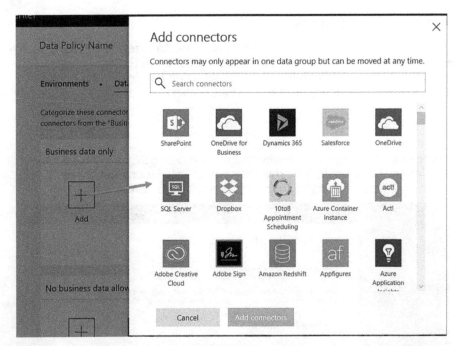

Click on the plus sign in one of the groups to add services to that group. Click on 'Save Policy' when enough services have been added.

5   IMPORTANT CONCEPTS

In this chapter I will explain some concept that you must understand or at least recognize when you continue reading this book. If my explanations below are too theoretical at this stage, return to this chapter when you actually start building your own flows. Then you will surely come to understand the meaning of each bold word below.

The principle of flow creation (all other automation) is that you select actions to be taken. You can also set conditions for the actions, so that they are only performed when these conditions are met. A predefined trigger decides when the process should start. Trigger, actions and conditions are selected from a range of options when the flow is created.

A flow is built with connectors, a trigger, condition(s) and action(s). You create the flow by combining these components in a way that gives the result you require. Inside conditions and actions you can use dynamic content, expressions and hardcoded text.

Example:

A flow with the **connectors** SharePoint and Outlook can have the **trigger** 'SharePoint - When an item is created'.

The **condition** can be that the SharePoint item must have the Priority field set to 'High'. If the condition is true, the **action** can be to send an e-mail message via Outlook to the assignee. If the condition is not true (and the priority is Normal or Low) no action is specified. This means that the flow will only send e-mails when the priority field has the value "High".

The e-mail that is sent when the task has high priority, has some **dynamic content**: the receiver of the e-mail, the name of the new task and a link to the task. This content is fetched from the new SharePoint item and is different in each e-mail. The e-mail can also have **hard-coded text**.

Flows are created online, in a Flow Editor on the Flow site. The editor is displayed when you have selected the trigger, and then you can build the flow step by step. You will learn much more about that in the next chapter.

5.1   CONNECTORS

A connector is most often a cloud based data source that is used in the flow. A flow can fetch data from the connector, perform actions with the help of the connector and even change connector data.

There are also connectors that do not require that you connect to any other system than Microsoft Flow, like Approvals, Control, Date Time, Notifications, Schedule and Variables. Some of these connectors do not show up on the Connectors page in the Flow site, but you can search for them in the Flow Editor and they are often very useful.

Most flows have 1-4 connectors.

You can see most of the connectors that you can use with Flow under the 'Connectors' tab in the Flow page. I suggest that you filter the connectors by "Standard connectors", instead of the default "All connectors", because the "All connectors" option shows the Premium connectors that are only available for subscribers to a Plan.

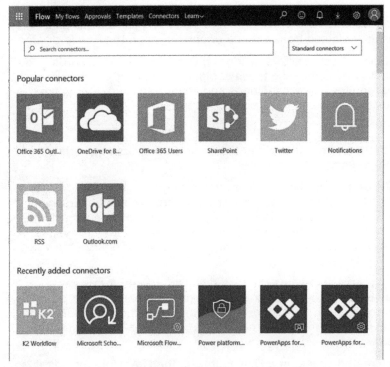

The first time you connect to an online service from the Flow site, you might be asked to log in to it.

Other services do not require login, and then you can just click on 'Continue' to connect to these services.

After the first time, you will be connected automatically to these services. A green arrow confirms that there is a connection.

This flow will connect to:

	Office 365 Outlook	PeterK@kalmstrom.com
	View permissions	⋯
	SharePoint	PeterK@kalmstrom.com
	View permissions	⋯
	Office 365 Users	PeterK@kalmstrom.com
	View permissions	⋯

5.1.1   From Template

When you start building a flow from a template, you will directly see the connectors used in the flow. The images in the section above show such information under 'This flow will connect to'.

5.1.2   From Blank

When you start creating a flow from scratch, instead of using a template, you will be asked to select one of the connectors. (Once again I recommend the Standard filter to hide Premium connectors)

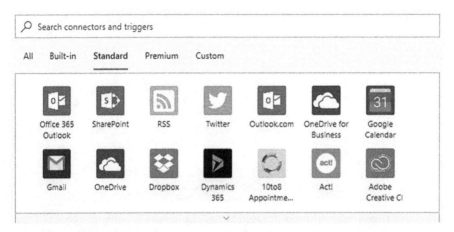

Later in the flow creation, you can add more connectors to the flow.

5.1.3 Approvals

The Flow site has an entry for Approvals in the left pane, and there are several templates for different kinds of approvals. Approval requests can be seen and answered directly on the Flow site, in a mobile or by e-mail.

5.1.3.1 Request sign-off

When a list or library has approvals enabled, it is possible to run an approval flow for a selected a file or item directly from the app – if it has the modern interface with the Flow button.

'Request sign-off' adds a 'Sign-off status' column to the app and lets you run a flow that sends an e-mail to the approver.

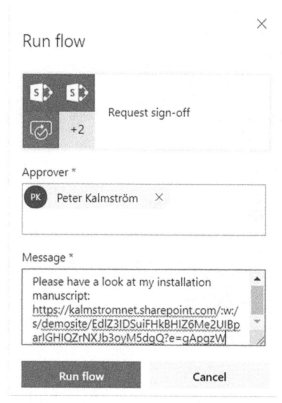

Chapter 9, Approval Flows, has information on how to create example flows that send approval requests automatically, and in chapter 10, Get E-mail Input on New Items, I describe another flow that also can be used for approvals.

5.1.4   Schedule

The Schedule connector has only one trigger, 'Recurrence', *refer to* 5.2.3, Recurrence, and two actions, 'Delay' and 'Delay until', *refer to* 5.3.3, Delay a Flow.

5.1.5   Variables

A variable is like a container that holds different types of information, and you can use variables for storing, modifying and retrieving any kind of data.

The benefit of using a variable, is that you can set the value of it once, and then reuse that variable whenever needed. To use a variable in Flow, you first have to initialize it.

To initialize a variable, add the action 'Variable – Initialize variable' into your flow, set the variable name, type, and set the value.

The image below shows a simple example, where I have set the task Title to the the dynamic content 'Filename with extension'. Then I have used the variable in an action for a tasks list.

This is convenient, because when I use this variable for several tasks they will all have the same format. And if I want to change something, I just have to change it once – in the variable.

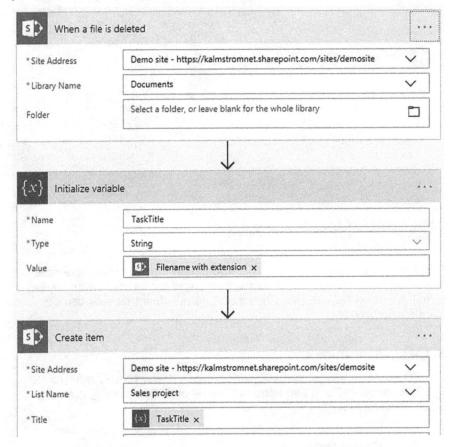

Note that I have not renamed the variable action here, but you should do that, especially if you use several variables.

I have written the name in CamelCase style here, even if it is not necessary in Flow, because it is necessary in programming languages and other places where variables are also used so it is a good habit to learn.

The Variables connector has several actions and can be used for various types of data. To see example flows that use variables, *refer to*:

Chapter 13, Monthly Projects Report

Chapter 24, Send E-mails with Attachments from a Shared Mailbox

5.1.6   Button

The Button connector is included in several templates and can also be selected by a blank flow. This connector is intended for the Flow mobile app, and it adds a button to manually run a flow in the mobile device. It is used for simple, personal flows but Microsoft is planning similar buttons for SharePoint apps that can be interesting for business flows.

5.2   TRIGGER

The trigger decides in general when the flow should be run. A SharePoint flow trigger is most often started automatically when the trigger is performed, but there is a certain delay on up to five minutes.

A typical SharePoint trigger is "when an item is created". This trigger gives the dynamic content 'ID', as opposed to "when a file is created", so I often use the "item" trigger even if the flow runs in a document library. In that case the document library name cannot be chosen. You have to enter it as a custom value.

Whether you use a template or a start with a blank flow, you must specify which SharePoint site and app you want the flow to connect to for the trigger. Sometimes you can or must also specify other parameters.

5.2.1   Template Trigger

When you start creating a flow from a template, the trigger is chosen for you. As the templates are named after what they do and not after the trigger, you don't see the trigger until the flow is opened in edit mode.

5.2.2   From Blank Trigger

When you start the flow from blank, some popular triggers are displayed.

If none of the most popular triggers is suitable for your flow, click on 'Search hundreds of connectors and triggers'.

Search for and select a connector, and triggers for that connector are displayed below the connector selection. Scroll down or search among them to find the one you want.

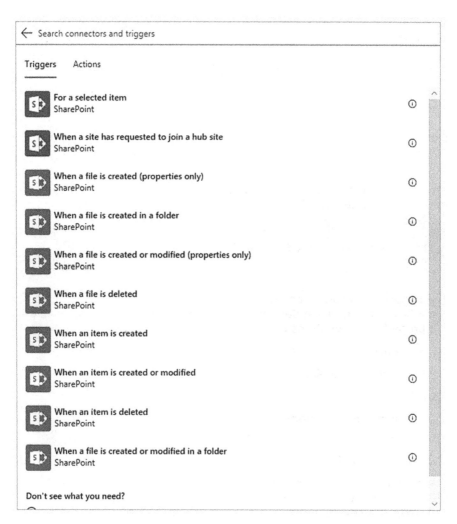

← Search connectors and triggers

Triggers   Actions

For a selected item
SharePoint   ⓘ

When a site has requested to join a hub site
SharePoint   ⓘ

When a file is created (properties only)
SharePoint   ⓘ

When a file is created in a folder
SharePoint   ⓘ

When a file is created or modified (properties only)
SharePoint   ⓘ

When a file is deleted
SharePoint   ⓘ

When an item is created
SharePoint   ⓘ

When an item is created or modified
SharePoint   ⓘ

When an item is deleted
SharePoint   ⓘ

When a file is created or modified in a folder
SharePoint   ⓘ

Don't see what you need?

You can also search for the trigger directly and have suggestions from different connectors.

5.2.3   Recurrence

Most triggers start a flow when something happens, for example when a new item is added to a list. But flows can also be run at certain times or with a certain frequency, and for that we use the trigger 'Schedule – Recurrence'.

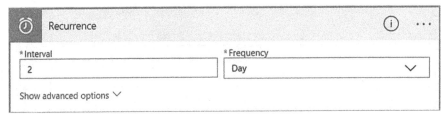

Flows that are set to run with a certain frequency run for the first time when you save it. Therefore you don't have to perform a trigger to test it – just check that the flow has given the preferred result.

After the first run, Recurrence flows will run at the interval you have set for them. They can also be run manually from the 'My flows' page.

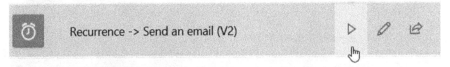

The Recurrence trigger can be used in reminders or when you want to run a flow that queries a data source and takes certain actions based on the properties of the items in the data source.

A Recurrence trigger is used in these example flows:

13, Monthly Projects Report

23.1, Event Reminder

23.2, Contract Review Reminder

5.3 ACTIONS

The action decides what parameters the flow should affect and what should be done with them. A flow must have at least one action, but it can also have several actions, defined in different steps.

Actions are built with text, dynamic content, expressions, URLs and whatever is needed to be put in the various fields. You will learn much more about that in the example flows further on in this book.

Select the action by first searching for and selecting the connector.

When you have selected the connector, you will have a range of actions to choose from. You can also search for the right action directly.

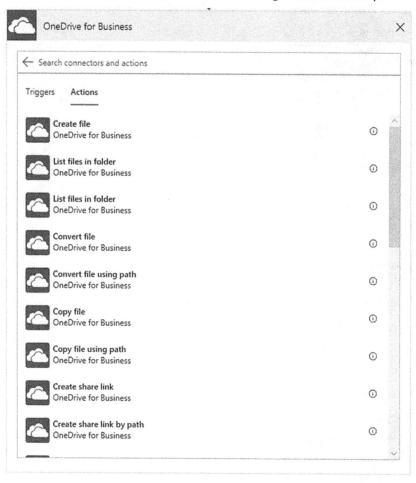

The details of the action is defined in the flow's action step, and each selected action gives different options for the action step. For example, when the action is to send messages, the action part can define the receiver, subject and body text of these messages. (For that information we often use dynamic content, *refer to* 5.5, Dynamic Content.)

Flow has a lot of actions to select from. Actions can also be combined with conditions so that actions are performed only under certain conditions or different actions are performed for different conditions.

For each SharePoint action, you must specify which SharePoint site and app you want the flow to connect to for the action. Often you also can or must specify other parameters, and for some actions even flows that start from blank have default values that you might want to remove or change.

5.3.1 Conditions

A condition is actually a Control action. A condition limits another action, so that a certain condition or certain conditions must be met for the action to take place. The condition has two options, Yes or No, and from that you can build different scenarios depending on which option is true.

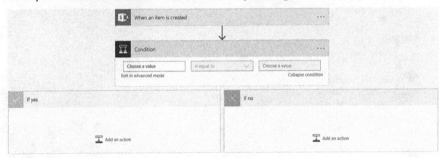

Often only the 'If yes' option is used, as no action is required when the condition is not true. In this case, that part of the flow is only performed when the condition is true.

Conditions are used in many of the example flows:

9.1, Approval with the Built-in 'Approval Status' Column

9.2, Approval with a Custom Approval Status Column

12, Progress Bar

16, Roll Back Column Changes

19, Copy Survey Responses from Forms

21.1, New Employee Tasks without a Settings List

23.1, Event Reminder

5.3.2   *Apply to Each*

The action 'Apply to each' is another Control action that loops through collections of data. You can for example use this action to process items in a SharePoint list.

You can find 'Apply to each' by searching for it among the actions.

Use loops when you want to go through many items and check or do something with each of them. First add the 'Apply to each' and then add new action(s) within that action.

Select how you want the result of the 'Apply to each' action to be output. Most often the output is set to the dynamic content 'value'.

Note that the new action should be added inside the 'Apply to each' action, with the 'Add an action' button. When you are finished with the 'Apply to each', you can add more actions by clicking on 'New step' as usual. Those actions will NOT be performed on each item. The 'Apply to each' container box is important.

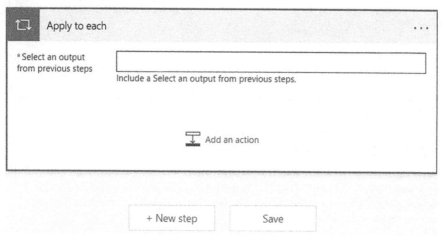

'Apply to each' actions are very useful, so they are included in all these example flows:

13, Monthly Projects Report

17, Set Task Assignee Depending on Category

19, Copy Survey Responses from Forms

21.2, New Employee Tasks with a Settings list

23.1, Event Reminder

23.2, Contract Review Reminder

24, Send E-mails with Attachments from a Shared Mailbox.

29

5.3.3   Delay a flow

Flows are normally run within five minutes after the trigger has been performed, but with a delay action you can set the flow to be run at a specific time after the trigger. Find the two delay actions by searching for the Schedule connector:

- 'Schedule – Delay', where you specify a number and a time unit. With this action you can for example delay the flow run for 10 minutes.

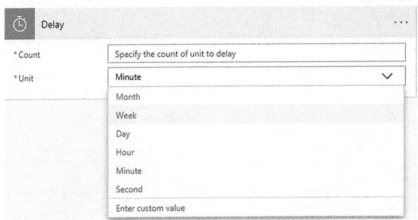

- 'Schedule – Delay until', where you specify a date and time when the flow should be run.

5.3.4   E-mail Actions

Flow generated e-mails will by default have the flow creator as sender. If you want to avoid that, you can use the action 'Mail – Send an email notification'. This action acts as its own Flow based connector. The e-mail sender will look like this:

Microsoft PowerApps and Flow <microsoft@powerapps.com>

This action is good for simple notification e-mails, but you miss some features that present in "Office 365 Outlook" actions, such as options and rich text.

To take advantage of the "Office 365 Outlook" actions, you can use a shared mailbox where the flow creator account is a delegate.

5.4   HARD-CODED TEXT

The easiest way to decide what value a parameter should have in a flow is to write it directly in the Flow Editor. This is called to hard-code, because the method always gives the same result.

Hard-coding is useful if you for example want some general text in a flow generated e-mail, like "You have received a high priority task". Then this text will be the same in all e-mails that are sent by this flow.

But when you want to add the name of the task, or a link to it, you must use dynamic content, *see* below. If you hard-code the task name or link, the flow can only be used for one task!

Hard-coding has a serious drawback: if a parameter value is changed, you have to modify the flow. Therefore you should always think twice before you hard-code. In chapters 17 and 21, I show how hard-coding can be avoided by using a settings list.

5.5 DYNAMIC CONTENT

When you add dynamic content in flow fields, the content in actions changes depending on what happens in the connectors. Dynamic content can be selected from a list that is displayed to the right when you click in a flow field. (If you have a small screen, the dynamic content can also be displayed below the field, but then there is no search option.)

The dynamic content is fetched from the connectors, and what is shown as suggestions depends on the action. In the image below, the mouse cursor is placed in the 'To' field of the 'Send an email' action, so different options for the receiver of the e-mail are suggested as dynamic content for that field.

Search, or click on 'See more' above the suggestions if you cannot find the dynamic content you are looking for.

Dynamic content is shown with the connector icon and can be removed by the x in the right corner.

The dynamic content is grouped by the flow's trigger and actions, so sometimes the same name for a dynamic parameter can be present in several groups. Make sure you select the right one!

Note that you sometimes have to set a dynamic value for a field even if you don't want the flow to change anything in it. This happens when a

31

field is mandatory, and in those cases you just set the same dynamic value as the field name.

5.6 EXPRESSIONS

Expressions can be compared to functions, procedures or methods in traditional programming languages, but you don't have to be a programmer to use expressions. Microsoft has given a lot of expressions that you can use, and both the actual expression syntax and a description of what the expression achieves is displayed under the Expressions tab in the Flow Editor.

You can search among the expressions just like you do with the dynamic content. You can also start writing in the function field and then select a suitable parameter from the IntelliSense suggestions you get.

Dynamic content can also be included in expressions. Click on 'Dynamic content' while you are building your expression and include content from there. It will be added to the expression with the correct syntax.

Expressions are used in several of my example flows, and for each expression I will explain the steps to get the correct expression:

11, Calculate Totals

12, Progress Bar

16, Roll Back Column Changes

23.2, Contract Review Reminder

24, Send E-mails with Attachments from Shared Mailbox

5.6.1   Add the expression to the flow

When you have finished building the expression, put the mouse cursor on the place where you want to add it and click on the OK button under the expression.

If the expression should be added to other content in a field, be careful where you put the cursor so that you get the expression in the right place. Note that pressing the enter key is not enough – you have to press the OK button for the expression to be saved.

6 START CREATING A FLOW

Now it is almost time to really start building a flow, because that is what we will do at the end of this chapter. But first you need to learn how to start.

When you create a flow, you can either start with a template or start from scratch with a blank flow (which I often prefer to do to have a cleaner flow with better control.) You can also import an existing flow and modify it. All three options are available under 'My flows' on the flow site.

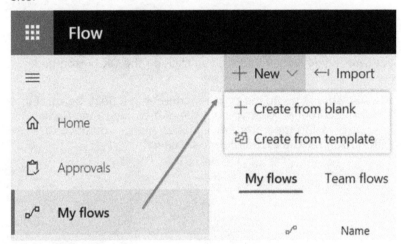

The template option can also be selected from a modern SharePoint list or library or from the Flow homepage.

If you select to use a template for the flow, you actually also select the trigger. When you start from blank, your first step will be to select a trigger.

6.1 THE FLOW SITE

Flows are managed online, at https://flow.microsoft.com. This site gives you access to many Flow templates and also a blank template, and here you can also see and manage the flows you already have created.

On the Flow site you can:

- create new flows from blank or from a template
- turn flows on or off
- edit flows
- have information about flow history
- delete flows

- export and import flows

- see connectors

- manage approvals

- reach tutorials.

6.1.1   Reach the Flow Site

Flows are always created on the Flow site at https://flow.microsoft.com. You can go directly to the site in your browser, by writing or pasting in the URL or by using the Flow button in the Office 365 App Launcher. This is the only option if:

- You want the flow to monitor a SharePoint list or library that has the classic user interface.

- You want to start with a blank flow. I often prefer to start with a blank flow, as it gives me better control. Therefore, you will see several examples on that in this book.

- You want to import an existing flow.

6.1.1.1   From SharePoint Online

When you use SharePoint Online, you can start creating a flow directly from the list or library that you want to apply the flow on. OneDrive for Business, which is a limited SharePoint Online site, also has a Flow button.

Make sure you have the modern interface, so that you can see the Flow button in the command bar. (If you cannot use the modern interface, go to the Flow site as described above.)

1. Click on the Flow button in the command bar and select 'Create a flow'.

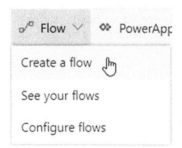

2. A pane where you can select a template for the flow will be displayed to the right. The choice of templates is limited to templates where SharePoint is one of the connector services.

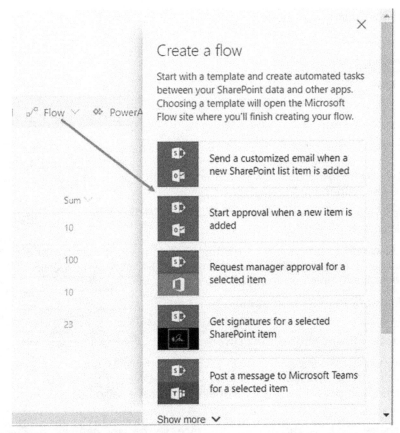

3. Select one of the templates or click on 'See more templates' (which becomes visible when you have clicked on 'Show more'). Now you will be directed to the Flow site, where you can either continue building the flow on a template or start building a flow from scratch.

When you select 'See your flows' from the dropdown, the 'My flows' page on the Flow site will open. When you select 'Configure flows', a right pane will open where you can enable or disable approvals for the app.

6.2 START FROM A TEMPLATE

If you have not selected a flow template in SharePoint, you can find a suitable template on the Flow site. There you can:

• search for a template

• select a template from the categories

• select a connector and then select one of the templates that are available for that service.

When you have selected the most suitable template for your flow, you will be presented with the online services that are included in the flow. Sign in to them, if you are not already logged in.

Now you can fill out the details for the flow you want to create. They are of course different for each template, but be aware of the default values! You should not only specify your own site, list and similar but also check the parameters that have default values and change them if needed.

Most example flows in this book start from a blank flow, as I find those cleaner and easier to work with, but these example flows use a template:

9.1, Approval with the Built-in 'Approval Status' Column

9.2, Approval with a Custom Approval Status Column

20, Copy Requested Dropbox Files to SharePoint

6.3 START FROM BLANK

Most of my example flows are created from blank instead of from a template, as I find that it gives better control over the flow.

When you use a template, the connector(s) and trigger are always chosen for you, but with a blank flow you must start with selecting a suitable connector and trigger.

Start building your flow by selecting 'New' and then 'Create from blank' under 'My flows' on the Flow site. (The 'Team flows' option that you can see in the image below is described in chapter 7, Share a Flow.)

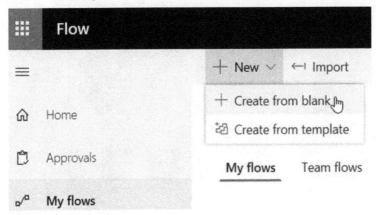

6.3.1 Choose Connector and Trigger

When you have selected 'Create from blank' under 'New' in the 'My flows' page, a new page will open. Here you have three options:

- Click on 'Create from blank' again.
- Select one of the popular triggers. The icon to the left of the flow description shows which connector is needed for the first step.
- Click on the Search button at the bottom of the page to find a suitable connector and trigger.

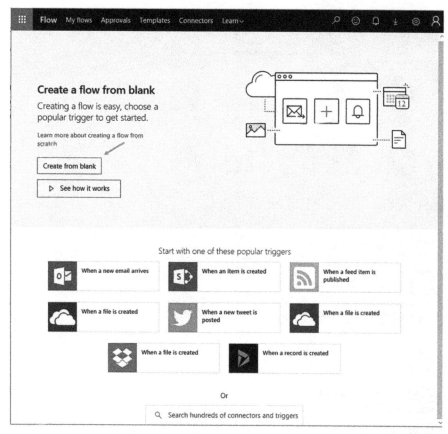

When you click on one of the popular triggers, the Flow Editor described in next section will open directly.

When you choose one of the other two options – the 'Create from blank' button or on the Search button – you will be directed to a page where you can select a connector and a trigger.

If you click on a connector icon, you will see all available triggers for that connector. You can also directly search for a trigger or choose one of the suggestions below the connector icons.

6.4 START FROM AN EXISTING FLOW

If you already own a flow that is similar to the one you want to create, you can use the 'Save as' feature. This will add a copy of the original flow to your 'My flows' page, and you can edit it as you wish. The copy is disabled by default, so it does not start running until you enable it. When you have edited, saved and tested the new flow, you can turn it on.

Both 'Save as' and 'Turn flow on' can be found under the ellipsis for each flow. In the image below, I have copied a Recurrence flow with 'Save as', and then I have clicked on the ellipsis at the copy.

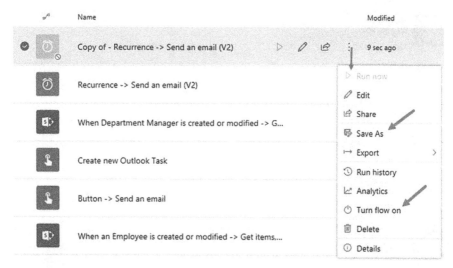

	Name						Modified
✔	Copy of - Recurrence -> Send an email (V2)	▷	✎	⬈	⋮		9 sec ago
	Recurrence -> Send an email (V2)				▷ Run now		
					✎ Edit		
	When Department Manager is created or modified -> G...				⬈ Share		
					🖫 Save As		
	Create new Outlook Task				↦ Export	>	
					🕔 Run history		
	Button -> Send an email				⌁ Analytics		
					⏻ Turn flow on		
	When an Employee is created or modified -> Get items....				🗑 Delete		
					ⓘ Details		

You can also start from an existing flow by importing a flow, *refer to 7.2.2, Import a flow.*

6.5 BUILD THE FLOW

Flows are built in a Flow Editor with boxes where you select suitable actions. The steps in the Flow Editor vary with each flow.

The image below shows a flow template where default values are added. When you have started the flow from SharePoint, the site and app where you clicked on the 'Flow' button are already entered.

The default values can of course be edited. Open and close each step by clicking on the top banner with the step name.

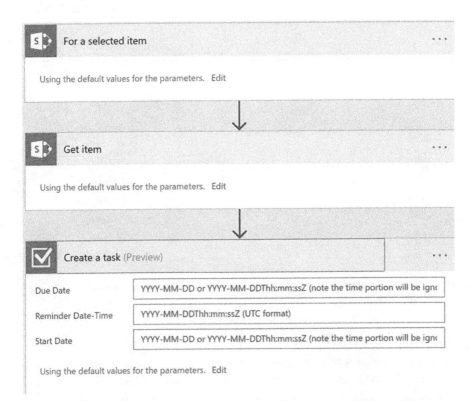

When you have chosen a blank flow with a SharePoint trigger, next step is to define the site and list, library, folder etc. that the flow should monitor.

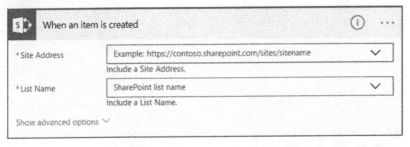

You can either select the site URL and app name or choose 'Enter custom value' and write or paste in the value. In some cases there is no selection, and then you can enter the values directly without selecting 'Enter custom value'.

Some SharePoint flow templates and triggers are intended for lists and some for libraries, but you can use them for both types anyway. The only limitation is that you might not be able to select the list or library. Instead you can select 'Enter a custom value' and write in the name of the list/library.

6.5.1   *Renaming*

I strongly recommend you to rename the titles of the boxes in the Flow Editor, so that the steps are easy to follow for other people who might edit the flow. Click on the ellipsis at the title and select 'Rename'.

I also suggest that you use CamelCase naming, *refer to* 2.3 CamelCase Naming, or underscore in the names but not spaces. Then you can use these names in other places in the flow.

You should also give the flow itself a good name. Click on the default name in the top left corner and write a more descriptive name than the default one.

Note: In this book I have *not* renamed anything, even though I advise you to do it, because I want the images to have the original names of triggers, actions and conditions. Otherwise my steps might be difficult to follow.

6.6   NEW STEP

After each step in the Flow Editor you can move to the next step with the 'New step' button. Now you can search for the action you prefer or pick it directly from the list.

+ New step

When you have clicked on the 'New step' button below an existing trigger or action, that box will be closed automatically. Click on the top banner to open it again.

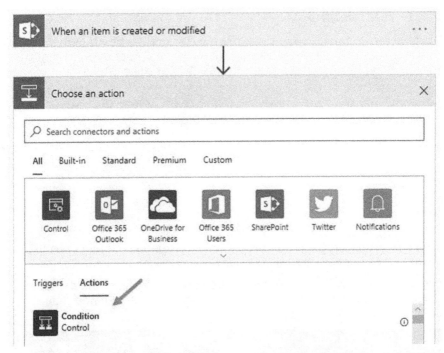

(The 'New step' button earlier gave three blue buttons: Action, Condition and More. You can see this in my demos, as Microsoft changed the user interface at the end of 2018.)

6.7   CREATE YOUR FIRST FLOW – SEND SKYPE MESSAGE ON NEW TASK

I will continue with more Flow theory later in this book, but I think you will understand everything better if we create one very simple flow to get the idea.

I have chosen a flow that sends a Skype message to a person who has been assigned a new SharePoint task – similar to my example above but without the condition. This flow is run automatically every time a new item is created in the SharePoint tasks list.

The flow includes two connectors, SharePoint Online and Skype for Business. When a new task has been added to the SharePoint list specified in the Flow Editor, the flow will run and send a Skype message to the person who has been assigned the new task. We will also include a link to the new list item in the message.

Connectors: SharePoint Online, Skype for Business

6.7.1 Prerequisites

A SharePoint list called *Sales Tasks*.

6.7.2 Theory

The site URL is often needed in SharePoint flows. The best way to get the site URL, is to right click on the icon in the top right corner in the site you want to use and select 'Copy link address'.

That will give you the correct URL for the flow. It is shorter than the URL in the address field, which also includes the specific page.

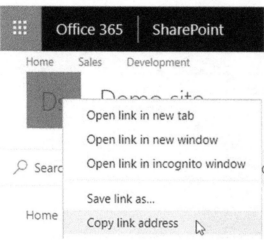

6.7.3 Steps

In this first flow I will be more detailed than in the example flows later on in this book. Many steps are the same in all flows and don't need to be repeated, for example that you first add the SharePoint site URL and then the app.

1. Go to the Flow site at https://flow.microsoft.com/ and create a blank flow.

2. Select the trigger 'SharePoint – When an item is created'. (Use the Search feature if you cannot see this trigger among the popular ones.)

3. Sign in with your SharePoint account, to create a Flow connection to SharePoint.

4. Select the SharePoint site URL. If you cannot see the site you want to use, select 'Enter custom value' and write or paste in the URL.

5. Select the *Sales Tasks* list, or enter its name as a custom value.

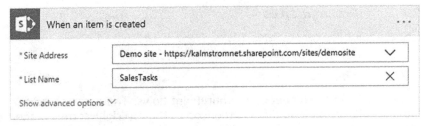

6. Click on 'New step'.

7. Write "Skype" in the search field to show all Skype for Business actions.

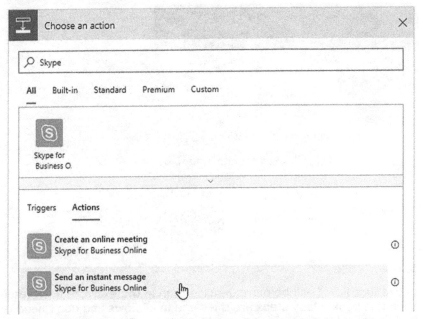

8. Select the Skype for Business action 'Send an instant message'.

9. Sign in to your Skype for Business account, to create a Flow connection to Skype for Business.

10. Create a template for the message:

   a. At 'To', add the dynamic content 'Assigned to Email'.

   b. In the 'Message' field, add suitable text, like "You have a new task". Then add the dynamic contents 'Task Name' and 'Link to item'. (Subjects are seldom used in Skype messages, and it is not mandatory, so we don't write anything here.)

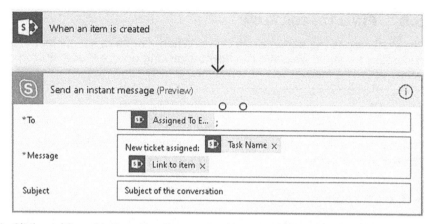

11. Click on 'Save' below the flow or in the top right corner to save the flow.

12. Click in the name in the top left corner and start writing, if you want to give it a more suitable name than the default one.

13. Click on 'Test' in the top left corner and select to perform the trigger action yourself.

6.7.4   *Test the flow*

To test the flow we created above, that sends a Skype message to a person who has been assigned a new SharePoint task, add a new task to the list where the flow should run.

1. Create a new item in the *Sales Tasks* list. Assign it to yourself or to someone for whom you can easily check the Skype conversations.

2. Make sure that a message is sent to the assigned person and contains the correct text, the task name and the link.

3. If there are problems, go back to the Flow site and edit the flow. Read the instructions above again, or watch the demo, and also study next section for information about testing and troubleshooting. I am sure you will find the error.

4. When you test again, you can use the option to use data from previous runs.

5. When the flow works as it should, check that you can find it under 'My Flows' in the Flow site. You might need to refresh the page to see it.

Demo:

https://www.kalmstrom.com/Tips/SharePoint-Flows/Flow-IM-Alert.htm

47

6.8 FINALIZE THE FLOW

The final step is the same for all flows. When you have set the actions necessary for the flow, save the flow by clicking on the 'Save' button below your last step or at the top right.

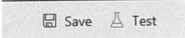

You can also directly click on the 'Test' button and then 'Save and Test', *see* the image below.

6.8.1 Test

When you have finished creating a flow, you should always test it by performing the trigger action. That way you can make sure it runs and gives the result you wished to achieve when you created it.

In the top right corner above the Flow Editor, there is a 'Test' button to click on. In the left corner above the Flow Editor, Flow will give you a hint what to do to test the flow.

ⓘ To see it work now, modify a list item in the SharePoint folder you selected.

For new flows only one test option is valid: 'I'll perform the trigger action'.

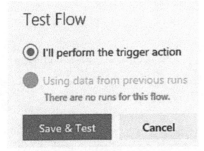

The second option can be used when you need to repeat the testing. That way, you don't have to perform the trigger action (for example create a new test item) for each test run. Select which run you want to repeat.

Test Flow   ✕

◯ I'll perform the trigger action

⦿ Using data from previous runs
Choose data from a list of previous runs:

⦿ ● Test Failed	22 seconds ago
◯ ● Test Failed	52 seconds ago
◯ ● Test Failed	3 minutes ago

When you have clicked on 'Save & Test', or just 'Test' if you saved the flow with the 'Save' button first, (and performed the trigger action if you have chosen that option) the information in the left corner will be replaced with run info.

ⓘ Your flow is running...   ✓ Your flow ran successfully.

6.8.1.1   Schedule flows

To test a flow that runs on a schedule, run it manually and make sure it has run successfully and has no error messages.

To run the flow, select it on the 'My flows' page and click on 'Run now' or on the play icon to the right of the flow name.

(Note that all flows cannot be run this way. It depends on the trigger if the Play button is there or not.)

6.8.1.2   Difficult triggers

If the trigger action is difficult to perform (such as filling out a time-consuming form), you can first create the flow with a more easily tested trigger and then replace the trigger when you have made sure that the flow works well.

6.8.2   Edit a Flow

To make changes in a flow, go to the Flow site and open 'My flows'. Now you can select a flow and click on the pen icon to edit it.

In SharePoint Online, you can also click on 'See my flows' in a modern list or library. That will take you directly to the 'My flows' page.

When a flow has been created, a new 'Edit flow' button will be visible to the right above the Flow Editor. You can also click on that button to edit the flow.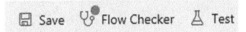

In all cases the Flow Editor will open in edit mode, and you can make your changes. When you are finished, save and test the flow again.

6.8.3   Troubleshoot a Flow

Microsoft Flow is rather good at giving hints at problems that prevent the flow from running as it should. There may however be problems in the flow even if no hints are given.

6.8.3.1   Errors while Building

When you are building the flow, the Flow Checker in the top right corner above the Flow Editor shows a red dot to indicate that the flow has a problem.

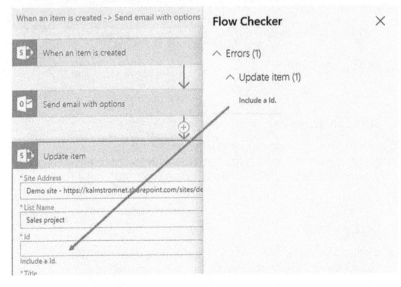

If you open the Flow Checker, the error will be explained.

Often you don't even have to open the Flow Checker, as red text under the field with the problem indicates what you should do to fix it.

When this is written, Flow has a bug in the Flow Editor that might be confusing. When you start writing a name in a 'To' field in an e-mail sending action and then select the receiver among the suggestions, there will be an error message that the e-mail is not valid. The message disappears when you remove the automatically added semi-colon after the name, and it does not affect the flow.

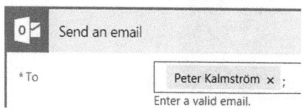

6.8.4   Errors while Testing

You cannot save and test a flow that has obvious errors that are indicated in red and by the Flow Checker, but sometimes the flow can be saved in spite of errors. Then the flow will fail, which you will see when you test it.

In the image below a red exclamation mark shows that the action 'Get items' failed. The 'Apply to each' was not performed because of that.

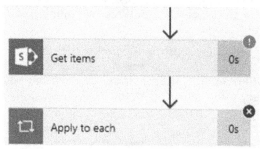

Now you can open the 'Get items' action and look for the error, which in this case was a missing space after 'eq', which gave 'eq5', in the Filter Query. Edit the flow to fix the error and test it again.

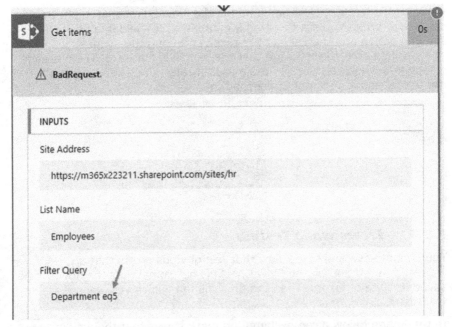

Another reason for a flow failure can be that you have selected the wrong dynamic content. If you search for a dynamic content, you will see that you sometimes get more than one hit with the same name, but from different parts of the flow.

You can see from the list which action created the dynamic content. In the screenshot below, both the 'Get items' action and the 'When an item is created' trigger has produced an output with the name ID. This can be confusing, and it is of course very important to choose the right one.

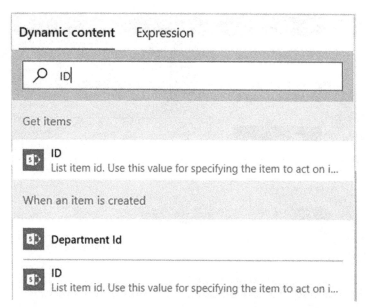

You can check if you have chosen dynamic content from the wrong group by hovering the mouse over it in the Flow Editor.

In the image below, the value of the Department column will be fetched from the item that triggered the flow: 'When an item is created'.

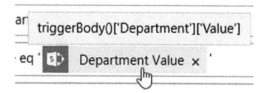

6.8.5 Errors while in Production

When a flow for some reason stops running, the notifications icon at the top of the web portal shows a message. The failed flow is shown if you click on the icon, and you can open it directly.

If you click on 'Show all activity' you will see all flows, but you can also filter the flows so that you only see failures.

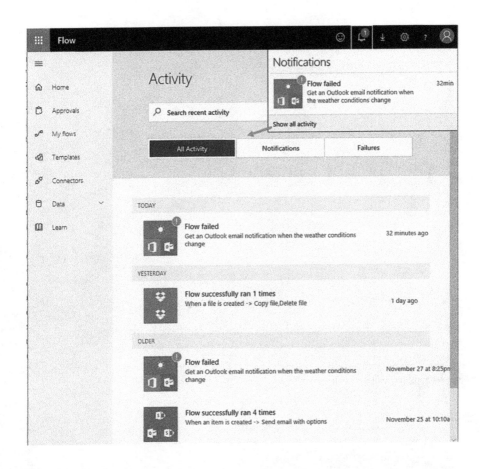

Finally, if the flow that has been working should stop running, the owners will be sent an e-mail messages about it. (This is of course a real benefit to Flow as compared to SharePoint workflows. Often the first notification an administrator would get of a failed workflow is when/if a user complains.)

7   SHARE A FLOW

There are two ways to share a flow with other users: making them owners to Team flows and export/import.

7.1   TEAM FLOWS

If flow creators use their personal accounts for business flows, it is important that they share the flow so that it can be managed by other people if the creator is absent or leaves the organization. Once a flow is shared, it is easy to distribute a link, pointing to the particular flow, to the Flow collaborators.

1. Go to 'My flows' and select the flow you want to share.

2. Click on the 'Share' icon or select 'Invite another owner' under the ellipsis.

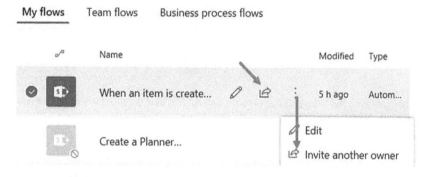

3. Add the user or group – or the SharePoint list or library – that you want to make owner of the flow.

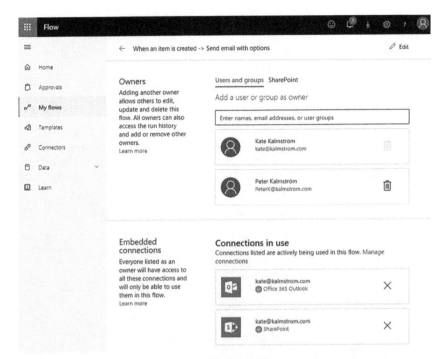

Note: when you add a SharePoint list or library as co-owner to a flow, everyone who has edit access to the list also gets edit access to the flow.

When you have shared a flow, it will no longer be visible under 'My flows'. Instead, you and all other owners can see it under 'Team flows'.

You should be aware that owners have considerable permissions over the flow. They have access to the connectors and to the content in the connected accounts, but only for the flow they share. They can modify and even delete the flow, and they can invite new people to share the flow and delete existing owners.

Owners can:

- view the flow run history
- manage the properties of the flow (for example, start or stop the flow or update credentials for a connection)
- edit the flow (for example, add or remove an action or condition)
- export the flow
- add and remove other owners, except the flow creator
- delete the flow.

If you don't want to grant all the permissions included in an ownership, you can instead export the flow to share it, *see* below.

7.2 EXPORT AND IMPORT FLOWS

The 'My flows' page gives a possibility to export and import flows. Both options are reached from the 'My flows' page on the Flow site. These features are primarily intended as an alternative way of sharing. If you just want a copy of a flow that you own, you can use the 'Save as' feature, *see* 6.4, Start from an Existing Flow.

Exporting and importing is also the way to copy flows between Office 365 tenants.

7.2.1 Export a flow

Flows can be exported as .zip or .json files.

1. Under 'My flows', click on the ellipsis at the flow you want to export and select 'Export'.

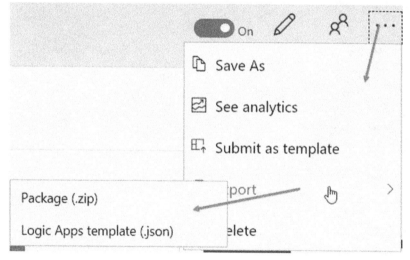

2. Select file format: 'Package (.zip)' or 'Logic Apps Template(.json)'.

3. Give the package a name and click on 'Export'.

4. Save the package to your computer.

The .json option gives a logic app than can be imported for example to Microsoft Azure, which is out of scope for this book. I will instead describe the .zip option in the import section below.

7.2.2   Import a flow

Import of flows may be done to update an existing flow or to create a new flow with an existing flow as a template. In both cases the first steps are the same:

1. Under 'My flows', click on 'Import' in the top left corner.

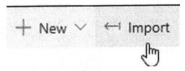

2. Upload the flow .zip package you want to import.
3. Review the package content.

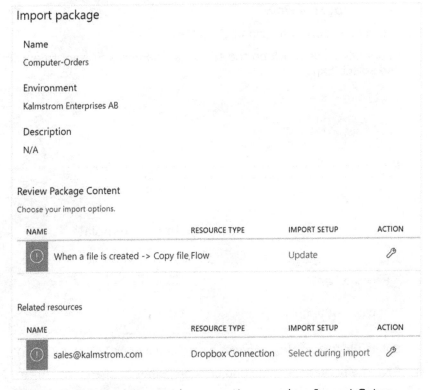

4. Click on the 'Action' icon to choose options, and an Import Setup pane will open to the right.

7.2.2.1   Update an existing flow

To update an existing flow is the default option in the Import Setup. Keep that option and select the flow you want to update among the existing flows.

Setup

Update	▼

The package creator chose this setup. You can make changes to the i
mport here.

The app or flow already exists in the environment and will be update
d when this package is imported.

NAME	RESOURCE TYPE
When a file is created -> Co py file,Delete file	2 mo ago
Move Video files	4 mo ago
Create a Planner task for a s elected item	2 mo ago

You also need to establish the required flow connector(s) under Related
resources.

Related resources

NAME	RESOURCE TYPE	IMPORT SETUP	ACTION
✕ sales@kalmstrom.com	Dropbox Connection	Select during import sales@kalmstrom.com	🖉

7.2.2.2   Create a new flow

When you have a flow that works well and want to create another flow
that is similar to the first one, you can re-use the first flow as a
template.

By importing a .zip package with the first flow, you don't have to start
from scratch with the new flow. Instead you can just change those flow
settings that should be different.

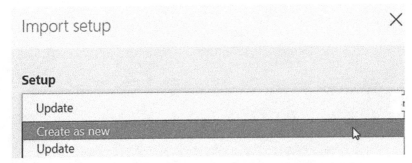

These are the steps to create a new flow by import:

1. Select the option 'Create as new' in the Import Setup.

2. Give the new flow another name than the original flow and save it.

3. Edit the related resources to establish the required connection(s), for example the SharePoint site.

4. Click on 'Import'.

5. Now the new flow is created, and you can find it under 'My flows'. It still has all the settings from the original flow, so you should edit the new flow and make any changes needed so that it works as you wish.

The example flow in chapter 18, Merge Orders into a Tasks List, shows how you can export and import flows.

EXAMPLE FLOWS

Now that you understand the basics about Microsoft Flow, I will give a number of example flows that you can try and of course modify for your own organization. Feel welcome to use them, or parts of them, or to just study them to understand the process.

All example flow descriptions are built in the same way:

- The **Prerequisites** sections give information about what I use in the flow. I have given lists and libraries example names, to make the flow steps easier to follow. These names are written in italics.

  Note that I only mention what is needed for the flow. For example, when I mention required SharePoint list columns, I only include those that I use in the flow – not other columns that might be needed for a meaningful list.

- In the **Theory** sections, I give pieces of general information that helps you understand the flow better. It is about Microsoft Flow, but I often also explain something about SharePoint Online that is relevant for understanding the flow. For general SharePoint information I however refer to my book *SharePoint Online from Scratch*.

- The **Steps** build on what you have learned in the previous chapters. I don't repeat how to perform basic steps like adding an action or saving the flow. That would make the descriptions unnecessarily long and boring, and you can always go back to the information earlier in the book.

  Instead, the Steps focus on what is special to the flow at hand, and I have tried to described those steps in detail.

8   SET DOCUMENT TITLES

Document titles are important for the SharePoint search results, but for many organizations it is a problem that library titles are missing or not accurate. This chapter introduces two flows that update file properties and set the title to the same as the file name.

Note that these flows will not help if users are not taught to change the default file names when they create new files inside a SharePoint library. Such files get a default name: Document, Book or Presentation, depending on file type, and if the creator does not change the default name, the library will eventually contain many documents with different contents but the same, non-descriptive names.

I suggest two trigger possibilities for this flow: 'SharePoint - when an item is created or modified' for existing SharePoint document libraries and 'SharePoint - when an item is created' for new libraries. The rest of the flows is the same for both options.

Connector: SharePoint

8.1   THEORY

When you have tried this flow I hope you will understand the importance of the SharePoint 'Title' column and the difficulties in getting relevant title values in SharePoint document libraries.

You should also know how to use triggers that are primarily intended for lists with a library.

8.1.1   *SharePoint*

The SharePoint Search displays title hits on top, so for the search to work well it is important that title columns in lists and libraries are filled out with terms that give relevant information.

In SharePoint lists, it is mandatory to fill out the title, and that is a good reason for re-naming that column instead of creating a new column for important information.

In SharePoint document libraries, however, users often don't enter anything in the title field, and that has several reasons.

- The title field is not mandatory in libraries.

- The title does not have the same importance in a file system as it has in SharePoint, so files that are imported into SharePoint libraries will often lack titles or have irrelevant titles.

- When you create a new SharePoint library, the title column is not visible by default.

8.1.2   Flow

The triggers 'SharePoint - when an item is created' and 'SharePoint - when an item is created or modified' are primarily intended for lists, so libraries do not show up in the Flow Editor dropdown for 'List' when you have entered the site URL. You can however select 'Enter a custom value' and then write in the library name.

The triggers will only give us the item, but to set the title we will also need the file properties. Therefore we have to fetch them with the action 'SharePoint – Get file properties' before we can set the flow to perform the actual update.

8.2   FLOW FOR EXISTING LIBRARIES

For an existing library, that already contains many files, it is best to use the trigger 'SharePoint - when an item is created or modified', so that you can have titles for all files in the library. The flow sets the title for new files, but with "modified" in the trigger it is also easy to update existing files by modifying all of them at the same time in edit mode.

8.2.1   Prerequisites

An existing *Procedures* SharePoint document library.

8.2.2   Steps

1. Create a blank flow and use the trigger 'SharePoint - when an item is created or modified' for the *Procedures* library.

2. Add the action 'SharePoint – Get file properties' for the *Procedures* library. In the 'Id' field, add the dynamic content 'ID' for the trigger item that was created or modified.

3. Add the action 'SharePoint – Update item' for the *Procedures* library:

    a. In the 'Id' field, add the dynamic content 'ID' for the item we got the file properties for.

    b. In the 'Title' field, add the dynamic content 'Name'.

4. Save and test the flow.

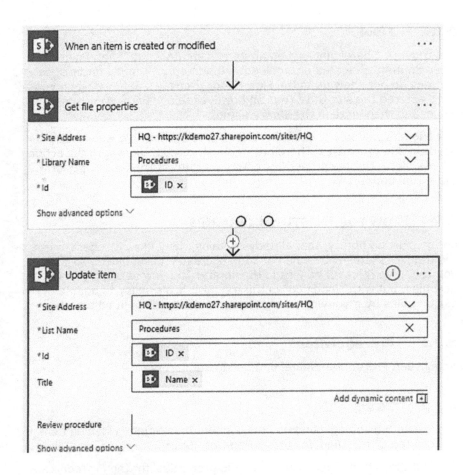

8.2.3   *Update Existing Files*

To update the titles of existing files, give them all the same dummy title. That is easily done with the library in edit mode: write a dummy title for the first file and drag the value down, like you can do in Excel.

Now all files are modified, so the flow will run and replace the dummy titles with the same as the file names.

Demo:

https://www.kalmstrom.com/Tips/SharePoint-Flows/Flow-Update-Title.htm

64

8.3   FLOW FOR NEW DOCUMENTS

For a new document library, or a library with only few files that can be updated manually, I would recommend the trigger 'SharePoint - when an item is created'.

With a "created" trigger, the flow will set the title to the same as the name for all new files, but the flow will not run when files are modified. Therefore, you can change any title manually, into something else than the name value, without having the flow thwart your modification.

8.3.1   Prerequisites

A new SharePoint document library.

8.3.2   Steps

To create a flow for new documents, use the trigger 'SharePoint - when an item is created'. From step 2 you can use the steps described above, in the flow steps for existing libraries.

Demo:

https://www.kalmstrom.com/Tips/SharePoint-Flows/Flow-Update-Title.htm

9   APPROVAL FLOWS

New or changed business documents must often be approved by someone else than the author before they are made available to more users, and that process can be managed in many different ways.

Microsoft has given a good descriptions on how to build an approval flow using the action 'Approvals - Start an approval', at https://docs.microsoft.com/en-us/flow/modern-approvals.

Microsoft has also given SharePoint users a possibility to run a flow from inside SharePoint to request approval, *refer to* 5.1.3.1 Request sign-off.

Here, I will show the difference if you use the Flow template 'Send approval email when an item is added' with a library that has the SharePoint built-in 'Approval Status' column, compared to using the same template with a library that has a custom column for approval status.

I will also show how to create an approval flow in the Flow mobile app.

Note that no request has to be done by the person who creates or uploads a file. These example flows send the e-mails automatically.

By default, the approval request will appear to come from the account that the creator was logged in with at creation and will be listed in that account's 'Sent requests' on the Flow site. Therefore, it is important to use the 'Requestor' field in the e-mail action, so that the person who actually created the document that triggered the flow will have the responses.

The flows work fine when files are uploaded to a SharePoint document library, but if a document is created directly in SharePoint the approval request will be sent the first time the file is saved. At that stage, the document is probably not finished, so a delay will be a good option for these flows. *Refer to* 5.3.3, Delay a flow.

For another example on an approval flow, *refer to* chapter 10, Get E-mail Input on New Items.

9.1   APPROVAL WITH THE BUILT-IN 'APPROVAL STATUS' COLUMN

This example flow sends an e-mail when a new item is added to a *Procedures* document library that has approvals enabled and thus an automatically added 'Approval Status' column. You can enable approvals under List/Library settings >Versioning settings.

The flow is easy to create, and it gives a nice e-mail where items can be approved. But the flow only sends an e-mail to the approver and then one with the result to the author of the document. The SharePoint library is not updated.

The image below shows the e-mail to the approver for the new file "Employee".

Approval Request: Employee

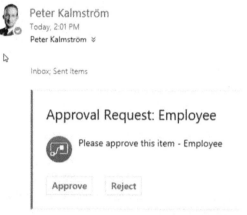

Connectors: Approvals, Office 365 Outlook, SharePoint

9.1.1 Prerequisites

A SharePoint *Procedures* document library where approvals has been enabled.

9.1.2 Theory

This example flow uses a library that has enabled approvals. It has certain benefits to do so, but there are also drawbacks.

9.1.2.1 SharePoint, built-in approval status column

When you enable approvals in a list or library, an 'Approval Status' column is automatically added to the app.

With approvals enabled, you can prevent other users than the author and the approver(s) from seeing the non-approved document versions. Not until the document has been approved, will it be visible to all users.

A drawback of using the built-in approval functionality, is that the approval is not registered as a modification of the item. This means that the approval is not shown in the document's version history, so there is no easy way to see who made the approval.

The built in 'Approval Status' column is not visible in the list/library settings. It cannot easily be customized and cannot be used in a Flow 'Update item' action.

9.1.2.2 Flow

In this flow we will use one of Microsoft's templates for approval flows. This template is primarily intended for list items, so we will change the default 'Title' to 'Name' in several places, as the name often is more appropriate in a document.

When this is written, the built-in 'Approvals Status' column cannot be combined with an "update item" action. Therefore, this flow does *not* update the status in the document library. It has to be done manually for each item.

When building flows that generate e-mails, I recommend that you first put your own e-mail address as receiver in the Flow Editor. When you have tested the flow and made sure that it works as it should, you can replace your e-mail address with the correct address.

9.1.3 Steps

This flow will send an approval request by e-mail and another e-mail to the person who created a new Procedure document.

1. Create the flow using the template 'Send approval email when an item is added'.

2. Add the *Procedures* library to the trigger, 'when an item is created'.

3. Fill out the action 'Start an approval':

   a. At 'Assigned To', enter the person who should approve.

   b. At 'Requestor', enter the dynamic content for the e-mail address of the person who created the item that triggered the flow, 'Created By Email'.

   c. At 'Details' keep or change the default text and add the dynamic content 'Name' instead of 'Title'.

   d. At 'Item link', add the dynamic content 'Link to item'

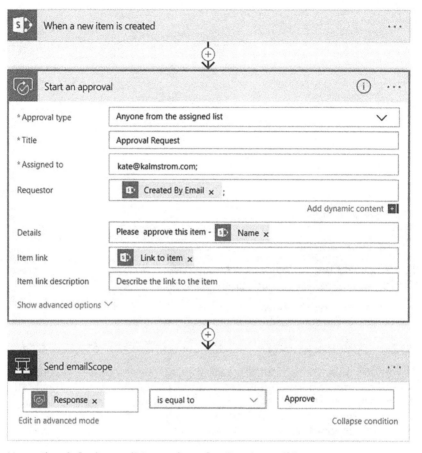

4. Keep the default condition values for Send emailScope.

5. If yes, fill out the action 'Send email':

   a. Keep the dynamic content 'Created By Email' in the 'To' field.

   b. Change 'Title' into 'Name' in the subject and body.

6. If no, add the action, 'Send email'. Use the same dynamic content as in the "If Yes" e-mail but change "approved" into "rejected".

7. Save and test the flow.

9.2 APPROVAL WITH A CUSTOM APPROVAL STATUS COLUMN

If you can manage without the security given by the built-in 'Approval Status' column, where no one can see the file or item until it has been approved, I recommend that you use a custom column for approval status. With such a column, you can expand the flow so that the status column is updated automatically when an item has been approved or rejected.

Connectors: Approvals, Office 365 Outlook, SharePoint

9.2.1 Prerequisites

A SharePoint *Procedures* document library with a choice column called "Procedure Approved" that is added to the default view. The options are Approved, Pending and Rejected. The default option is Pending.

9.2.2 Theory

In this flow we will use the same template for approval flows as in the flow above, so we will change the default 'Title' to 'Name'.

9.2.2.1 SharePoint, custom column for approval status

When you use custom approval status column, all users see the latest version of the document, even if it has not been approved. You can

70

however make it more difficult, by hiding the non-approved files from the default view.

The *Procedures* library in this example has two views: "All items", which includes non-approved files, and "Approved". The "Approved" view is default.

With a custom column for approval status, you can see in the version history when it was approved and by whom. In some business scenarios this is vital and required information:

Which doctor approved the drug for 2nd stage testing? Which engineer approved that this replacement part should be used? Which manager decided that the invoice should be sent to the customer?

9.2.3 Steps

Use the same steps as in the flow with the built-in approval status above, but add an action for update of the SharePoint list.

Steps 1-7, *refer to* the previous flow. (I recommend that you test also, before you continue with the library update.)

1. Under 'If yes', add the action 'SharePoint – Update item' for the *Procedures* library.

2. Set the 'Id' value to the dynamic content ID for the item that was added. Select 'Approved' at 'Procedure Approved Value'.

3. Under 'If no', add the action 'SharePoint – Update item' for the *Procedures* library.

4. Set the 'Id' value to the dynamic content ID for the item that was added. Select 'Rejected' at 'Procedure Approved Value'.

5. Save and test the flow.

Demo:

https://www.kalmstrom.com/Tips/SharePoint-Flows/Flow-Approvals.htm

9.3 APPROVAL FLOW IN A MOBILE

This flow is the same as the flow above, with a custom choice column for approval status. Therefore the theory and prerequisites are the same, but in the Flow mobile app I start with a blank flow and not with a template.

1. Log in to the SharePoint site that has the library where you want to use the flow. Press down on the SharePoint icon and copy the site URL.

2. Click on the plus icon to start with a blank flow.

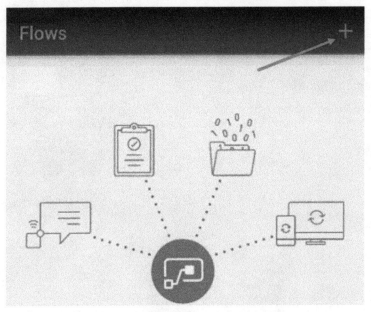

3. Use the SharePoint trigger 'When a file is created'.

4. Paste the site URL and select the *Procedures* library.

5. Add the action 'Approvals - start an approval'.

6. Add the dynamic content 'Name' at 'Title' and type the e-mail address of the approver. Also add the dynamic content 'Link to item'.

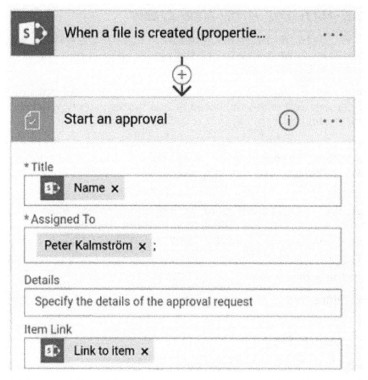

7. Add a condition: if the Response value is equal to 'Approved'.

8. Under 'If yes', add the action 'SharePoint - update file properties' and paste the site URL and select the library again. Select the dynamic property ID. At Approval value, select 'Approved'.

9. Under 'If no', add the action 'SharePoint - update file properties' and paste the site URL and select the library again. Select the dynamic property ID. At Approval value, select 'Rejected'.

10. Give the flow a name and save it.

11. Test the flow by uploading a file to the library.

Demo:

https://www.kalmstrom.com/Tips/SharePoint-Flows/Flow-Approvals-Android.htm

In next chapter, we will have a look at another kind of flow, that also can be used for approvals.

10 GET E-MAIL INPUT ON NEW ITEMS

Sometimes you need to have quick input from outside the tenant, and this example flow shows a way to get such input when a new item has been created in a SharePoint list.

The flow sends an e-mail with an item description and "vote" buttons to a specified person, and when the receiver has "voted" the flow sends the "votes" back to the list.

In this example, we imagine a legal department where the staff does not yet use SharePoint. Therefore they cannot open items and attachments in a SharePoint *Projects* list, but they still need to approve on new projects.

The example flow sends an e-mail to the legal department when a new project item has been created. The e-mail has a project description and three buttons: "Approved", "Rejected" and "Need More Info".

When the lawyer has clicked on one of the e-mail buttons, the flow adds the result to the Projects list.

Connectors: Office 365 Outlook, SharePoint

10.1 PREREQUISITES

A SharePoint *Projects* list with these columns:

- The 'Title' column is renamed to "Project Title".

- A multiple lines of text "Project Description" column.

- A single line of text column for the legal department's comment: "Legal Approval". This column is filled out by the flow and must not have a default value.

10.2 THEORY

Flow offers an action that creates an e-mail with option buttons. This flow example is primarily intended to show how this action, 'Office 365 Outlook – send email with options', can be used together with SharePoint.

This action is convenient to use when you want to ask for a quick input in cases where a form or something else more elaborate is not needed.

The example flow has three options, and the help text in the flow also shows three options, but the flow works with more or less options too. Each option is shown as a button in the e-mail.

E-mails generated by the flow action "Office 365 Outlook – Send email" by default has the importance set to 'Low'. You might want to change that!

10.3 STEPS

1. Create a blank flow and use the trigger 'SharePoint - When an item is created' for the *Projects* list.

2. Add the action 'Office 365 Outlook – Send email with options' and fill out the e-mail details:

   a. Receiver e-mail address.

   b. Subject: general text, for example "New project for approval" + the dynamic content 'Project Title'.

   c. Fill out the options, separated by a comma: Approved, Rejected, Need More Info.

   d. Under advanced options, add the dynamic content 'Project Description' in the body.

   e. Set 'Use only HTML message' to 'Yes'.

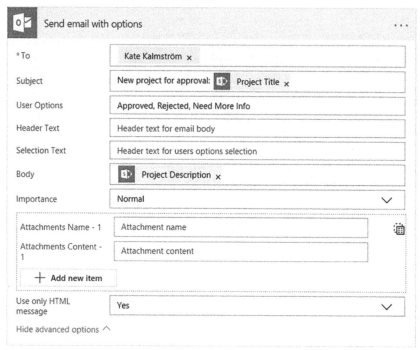

3. Add the action 'SharePoint – Update item' for the *Projects* list.

a. At 'Id', add the dynamic content 'ID' for the item that should be updated.

b. At 'Title', add the dynamic content 'Title' for the item.

c. At 'Legal Approval' add the dynamic content 'SelectedOption' from the send e-mail action. That will put the response from the Legal department in the SharePoint list.

d. Remove all the default options so that all other fields are blank.

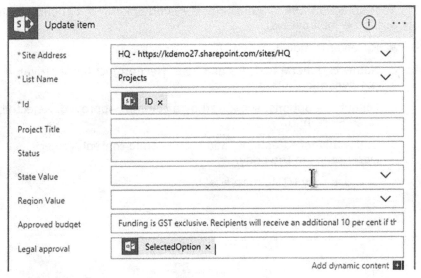

4. Save and test the flow.

Demo:

https://www.kalmstrom.com/Tips/SharePoint-Flows/Flow-E-mail-Input.htm

11 CALCULATE TOTALS

The 'Totals' feature can be used to summarize values in a SharePoint column, and the result of the calculation is shown on top of the column that is calculated. In the image below, the sums of hardware and setup costs have been calculated.

It is however *not* possible to use Totals for a column with calculated values, like the "Total Cost" column in the image, where the values have been calculated from the hardware and setup costs. I have pointed to the issue with a red line where the sum should have been.

⊕ **new item** or edit this list

	Title		Hardware Cost	Setup Cost	Total Cost
✓			**Sum= $1,700**	**Sum= $350**	▬▬
	Kalle's laptop ✳	•••	$500	$100	$600
	Stina's tablet ✳	•••	$400	$50	$450
	Bert's desktop ✳	•••	$800	$200	$1,000

To solve the problem, we can let a flow do the calculation and update the column. Then the "row sum" can have calculated values and the SharePoint 'Totals' feature can be used on the column.

This example flow calculates the sum of values in two currency columns and updates a third currency column. As we use a currency column for the result of the calculation – and not a calculated column – we can use the Totals feature without problems and see the Totals for the flow calculated column.

⊕ **new item** or edit this list

	Title		Hardware Cost	Setup Cost	Total Cost
✓			**Sum= $2,000**	**Sum= $550**	**Sum= $2,550**
	Kalle's laptop ✳	•••	$500	$100	$600
	Stina's tablet ✳	•••	$400	$50	$450
	Bert's desktop ✳	•••	$800	$200	$1,000

Connector: SharePoint

11.1 PREREQUISITES:

A SharePoint *Computers* list with the classic interface and three currency columns: "Hardware Cost", "Setup Cost" and "Total Cost". (The internal names are in CamelCase writing.)

The view should be modified so that all three columns use the Total Sum feature.

The values in the "Total Cost" column will be calculated by the flow.

11.2 THEORY

To understand this flow, you need to know the limitations of the Totals view and how a flow can use an expression to calculate the sum of column values.

11.2.1 SharePoint

Unfortunately the Totals feature can only be used in lists with the classic interface when this is written, but it will hopefully soon be added to modern lists too.

The Totals feature can not be used in columns that have calculated values.

11.2.2 Flow

In this example flow we will use an expression that calculates the sum of column values for a list item. You can create such an expression by entering the function 'add' and then the dynamic content for the columns that should be calculated. Separate the columns with a comma.

When you have done that, you will not see the dynamic content you have selected in the function field. Instead, Flow will give the expression that should be used, and you just have place the mouse cursor on the place where you want to insert the expression and click OK under the function field. Also *refer to* 5.6, Expressions.

11.3 STEPS

1. Create a blank flow and use the trigger 'SharePoint – When an item is created or modified' for the *Computers* list.

2. Add the action 'SharePoint - Update item' for the *Computers* list.

    a. At 'Id', add the dynamic content 'ID' for the created or modified item.

    b. At 'Title' add the dynamic content 'Title' for the item.

c. Create an expression for the 'Total Cost' field:

    i. Click on the Expression tab.

    ii. Start writing "add" in the function field, and select "add" when it comes up among the suggestions below the function field.

    iii. Add a parenthesis. The mouse cursor should come inside the parenthesis automatically, but if not, put it there.

    iv. Switch to Dynamic content and select 'HardwareCost'.

    v. Add a comma.

    vi. Select the dynamic content 'SetupCost'. Now you will have a finished expression.

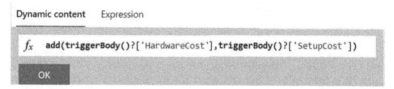

    vii. Place the mouse cursor in the 'Total Cost' field.

    viii. Click OK to the expression.

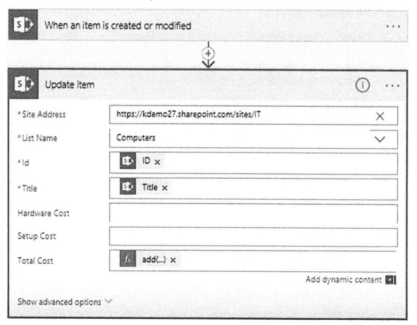

3. Save and test the flow.

Demo: https://www.kalmstrom.com/Tips/SharePoint-Flows/Flow-Calculation-Totals.htm

12 PROGRESS BAR

This example flow will add a progress bar to a *Tasks* list. It reads the value in the "% Complete" column and makes a graphic representation of that value in a separate column.

The technique I show here can be used whenever you want to add HTML code to a SharePoint list column, for example for conditional formatting.

Connector: SharePoint

12.1 PREREQUISITES:

- A SharePoint *Tasks* list built on the Tasks template. It has a custom multiple lines of text column called "Progress". The default formatting option for this column, 'Enhanced rich text', must be kept, and the column is added to the desired view.

- A piece of HTML code for the progress bar. The code used in the image above is:

  ```
  <table style="width: 100px; border: 0px">,
  <tr>
  <td style="padding: 0px; width: 100px; background-color: green"></td>
  <td style="padding: 0px; min-height: 16px; background-color: red"></td>
  </tr>
  </table>
  ```

  Note: "100" is marked bold above, because in the flow it will be replaced by dynamic content that calculates the required width.

12.2 THEORY

To understand this flow, you need to know how the "% Complete" column works in a SharePoint Tasks list and how its value can be used in a flow expression to calculate the completed part of the progress bar.

12.2.1   *SharePoint*

The SharePoint Tasks app template gives lists that have a checkmark box and a "% Complete" column with the default value of 0. When the box is checked, the value of the % Complete column will change to 100. Other values are set manually in the item form.

12.2.2   *Flow*

We use HTML code for a table with one row and two columns for the progress bar. The right column needs to have a min-height value, so that it is visible even if it has no content.

In this example flow, we will use an Expression that calculates the percentage of a column value. You can create such an expression by entering the function 'mul' and then add the dynamic content for the column that should be calculated within a parenthesis. Add ",100" before the end parenthesis and Flow will give the expression that should be used.

The 'mul' function performs the multiplication of the supplied parameters, in this case the column value and 100. The "% Complete" column is stored as a % number, that is a decimal between 0 (0%) and 1 (100%).

Example: a task that is halfway done would appear as 50%. In order for it to display as 50 pixels wide (half of the 100 pixels the progress bar is), we multiply the 0,5 by 100.

12.3 STEPS

The flow reads the value in the "% Complete" column and sets the width of the left column according to that value. The right column will be adjusted automatically, as the table has a fixed width of 100 pixels.

1. Create a blank flow and use the trigger 'SharePoint - when an item is created or modified' for the *Tasks* list.

2. Add the action 'SharePoint – update item' for the *Tasks* list.

    a. At Id, add the dynamic content 'ID' for the created or modified item.

    b. At 'Task Name', add the dynamic content 'Task Name' for the item.

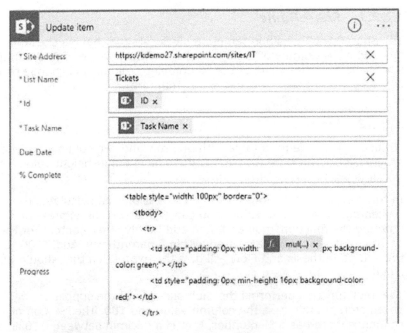

c. At 'Progress', enter the progress bar HTML code. Calculate the pixels needed for the width by replacing 100 in "width:100px" with an expression:

   i. Open the Expression tab and start typing "mul" in the function field, to multiply.

   ii. Enter a parenthesis.

   iii. Put the cursor inside the parenthesis and select the dynamic content "% Complete".

   iv. Add ",100" before the end of the parenthesis.

> f_x `mul(triggerBody()?['PercentComplete'],100)`

   v. Remove "100" after "width:" in the HTML code and keep the cursor at that place.

   vi. Click OK under the expression.

d. Remove the default entries in other fields so that all fields are empty except the ones you have filled out.

3. Save and test the flow.

Demo: https://www.kalmstrom.com/Tips/SharePoint-Flows/Flow-Progress-Bar.htm

13 MONTHLY PROJECTS REPORT

Managers often want to have monthly or weekly reports. This example flow will send an e-mail report that contains information about the total number of projects and the sum of the approved budgets for them. The flow will send this e-mail on the same day every month.

Connectors: Office 365 Outlook, SharePoint, Variables

13.1 PREREQUISITES

This flow takes information from a SharePoint *Projects* list. The list has the project name in the title column and a currency column, "Approved Budget".

The default view of the *Projects* list is called the 'All items' view.

13.2 THEORY

We use the 'Schedule – Recurrence' trigger in this flow, *refer to* 5.2.3. As such flows run automatically after they have been saved, you don't have to perform a trigger action to test this flow. Just check that it really sends the report and that it has the correct content.

In this flow we are using variables. Section 5.1.5 has general information about variables and explains one way of using them, but this flow will show another way.

The flow has two 'Initialize variable' actions, one for the total number of projects and one for the total approved budget. Both have numbers, but we will still need to use different types of variables.

The total number of projects cannot have decimals, so it will be an 'Integer'. The budget, on the other hand, is stored in a column that can have decimals, so even if you don't use decimals the type must be 'Float'.

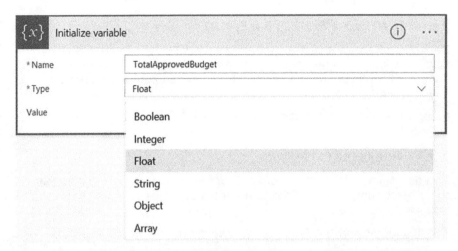

The values of these variables are calculated by two 'Increment variable' actions. They are executed inside an 'Apply to each' action that loops through the items in the *Projects* list.

In this flow I also introduce the Settings for an action. Most actions have such settings, different for each type, and here I use it to set a limit for a 'Get items' action. I set the limit very high, to make sure I really get all items.

I limit the action to only pick columns from one view, and the reason is that I want to make the flow run a bit faster.

13.3 STEPS

1. Create a blank flow and use the trigger 'Schedule – Recurrence'. Set the frequency to 1 month.

2. Add the action 'Variables – Initialize variable'.

    a. Set the 'Name' to "TotalNumberOfProjects".

    b. Set the 'Type' to 'Integer'.

    c. Leave the 'Value' field blank, as this value will be calculated by an 'Increment variable' action.

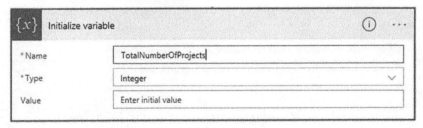

3. Add the action 'Variables – Initialize variable'.

a. Set the 'Name' to "TotalApprovedBudget".

b. Set the 'Type' to 'Float'.

c. Leave the 'Value' field blank, as this value will be calculated by an Increment variable.

4. Add the action 'SharePoint – Get items' for the *Projects* list.

   a. Click on the action ellipsis and select 'Settings'. At 'Limit', enter "5000" to be sure that you really get all projects.

   b. Under the advanced options, enter "5000" at 'Top Count', also to be sure to get everything.

   c. At 'Limit Columns by View', select the 'All items' view.

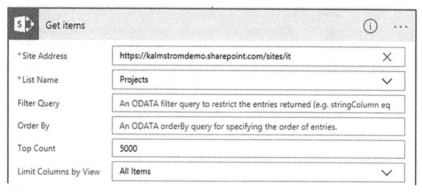

Get items		
*Site Address	https://kalmstromdemo.sharepoint.com/sites/it	✕
*List Name	Projects	⌄
Filter Query	An ODATA filter query to restrict the entries returned (e.g. stringColumn eq	
Order By	An ODATA orderBy query for specifying the order of entries.	
Top Count	5000	
Limit Columns by View	All Items	⌄

5. Add the action 'Apply to each' and set the output to the dynamic content 'value'.

6. Add the action 'Variables – Increment variable' for the 'Apply to each'.

   a. At 'Name' select the variable "TotalNumberOfProjects".

   b. Set the 'Value' to "1".

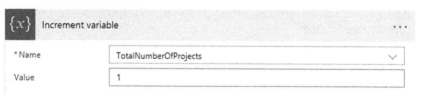

{x} Increment variable		
*Name	TotalNumberOfProjects	⌄
Value	1	

7. Add the action 'Variables – Increment variable' again.

   a. At 'Name' select the variable "TotalApprovedBudget".

   b. Set the 'Value' to the dynamic content 'Approved Budget'.

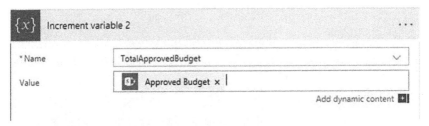

8. Add the action 'Office 365 Outlook – send an email' (outside the Apply to each) and fill out the e-mail details:

    a. Receiver e-mail address.

    b. Subject: general text, for example "Monthly project report".

    c. Body: explaining text + the dynamic contents from the Increment variables: 'TotalNumberOfProjects' and 'TotalApprovedBudget'.

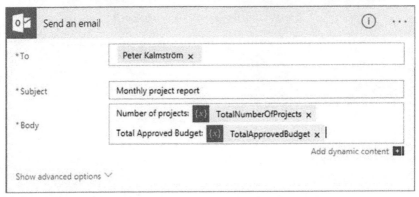

9. Save and check the flow.

Demo:

https://www.kalmstrom.com/Tips/SharePoint-Flows/Flow-Monthly-Projects-Report.htm

14 FORMAT E-MAIL BODY

In this example we will add a table to the body of a flow generated e-mail that is sent to a person when a new file has been added to a SharePoint *Procedures* document library.

The reason for the e-mail can be just information, or it can be an approval e-mail, but for this example the reason does not matter. Here we will just create an e-mail with a table in the body.

In each e-mail, the table is filled out with dynamic content for the file name and the creator of the new file.

Procedure name:	New customer
Created by:	Peter Kalmström

Connectors: Office 365 Outlook, SharePoint

14.1 PREREQUISITES:

- A SharePoint library, here called *Procedures*.

- HTML code for a table. Any style tags should be placed inside the body. Here is a suggestion:

```
<body>
<style type="text/css">
.auto-style1 {
width: 100%;
font-family:Verdana, Geneva, Tahoma, sans-serif;
font-size:small }
.auto-style2 {
        width: 255px;
        background-color: #99CCFF;}
</style>
<table class="auto-style1">
        <tr>
                <td class="auto-style2">Procedure name:</td>
                <td> </td>
        </tr>
        <tr>
                <td class="auto-style2">Created by:</td>
                <td> </td>
```

87

```
        </tr>
    </table>
    </body>
```

14.2 THEORY

Microsoft has recently added a new action to Flow: "Office 365 Outlook –
Send an email (V2)". It has a rich text HTML editor that allows changes
in font, style and color, as well as lists or links. More advanced HTML,
like tables and images, is not supported in this editor, but Microsoft has
announced an intention to add additional capabilities in the future and
also add rich text capability to more connectors and actions.

For now, however, the formatting options inside the Flow Editor are still
limited. A good option is therefore to use HTML code by copying code
that has been written in an HTML editor and pasting it into the Flow
Editor.

With the method I describe here, you can add for example tables and
images to the body of an automatic e-mail sent by a flow, or to the
description field in a SharePoint list item.

The code can be created in any HTML editor and pasted into the Flow
Editor. There you can add the dynamic content you want to use directly
in the code. There is however one thing you have to think about: tag(s)
that specify body code, for example style, should be placed inside the
body instead of in the head.

14.3 STEPS

1. Create a blank flow and use the trigger 'SharePoint – When a file is
   created (properties only)' for the *Procedures* library. (We don't need
   the actual documents to be included here.)

2. Add the action 'Office 365 Outlook – Send an e-mail'.

   a. Enter the recipient(s).

   b. Enter an e-mail subject.

   c. Click on 'Show advanced options' and select 'Yes' at 'Is HTML'.

   d. Go to your HTML editor and copy the style tag(s). Paste them into
      the body.

   e. In the HTML editor, copy the code in the body. (Do not include
      the two body tags.)

   f. Paste the code in the Flow Editor 'Body' field.

   g. Add dynamic content in the empty cell at 'Procedure name':
      'Name'

88

h. Add dynamic content in the empty cell at 'Created by': 'Created by DisplayName'.

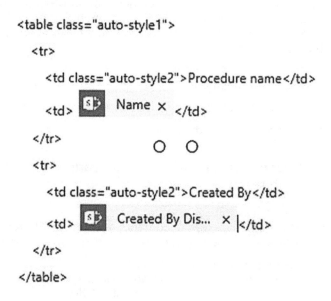

```
<table class="auto-style1">
   <tr>
      <td class="auto-style2">Procedure name</td>
      <td>  SP   Name ×   </td>
   </tr>
        O  O
   <tr>
      <td class="auto-style2">Created By</td>
      <td>  SP   Created By Dis...  ×  |</td>
   </tr>
</table>
```

3. Save and test the flow.

Demo:

https://www.kalmstrom.com/Tips/SharePoint-Flows/Flow-E-mail-Formatting.htm

15 E-MAIL LINKS

When you create a flow that sends an e-mail notification when a new item is added to a SharePoint list or library, you probably want to include some links in the e-mail body. Here I will give a few examples on how to build common links that point to the new item that has been created.

Note that these links might need a Plan, *refer to* chapter 3, Flow Plans.

When building links with dynamic content, you can choose two methods:

- Write in the link and select the dynamic content directly when the link is built.

- Paste a link without formatting and then replace parts of the link code with dynamic content.

Here are some useful links that open documents or items in different ways. Text within brackets in the link code represent dynamic content.

- A document in **preview** mode: <site URL>[Folder path]/Forms/AllItems.aspx? id=<site relative URL>/[Folder path] [File name with extension]&parent=<site relative URL>/[Folder path]

  Use this link when you don't want to invite users to edit the document. Note that 'AllItems.aspx' points to a view, and can be replaced with another view.

- A document or item in **edit** mode: [Link to item]

- **Document properties**

  o in display mode: <site URL><List Name>/Forms/Dispform.aspx? ID=[ID]

  o edit mode:
     <site URL><List Name>/Forms/Editform.aspx? ID=[ID]

- **List item properties**

  o in display mode: <site URL>/Lists/<List Name>/Dispform.aspx? ID=[ID]

  o edit mode: <site URL>/Lists/<List Name>/Editform.aspx? ID=[ID]

     Note that "Lists" is for English SharePoint versions. If you have another language, use the corresponding word in that language. For example, when you have a Swedish SharePoint you should use "Listor".

- The **Version history of a document**:

\<site URL\>/_layouts/15/Versions.aspx?FileName=\<site relative URL\>/[Folder path] [File name with extension]

- The **Version history of an item**: \<site URL\>/_layouts/15/Versions.aspx?/list=\<List ID\>&FileName=\<site relative URL\>/[Folder path] [File name with extension]

  Get the List ID by going into the list or library settings and copy the last part of the URL, after 'List='.

  ayouts/15/listedit.aspx?List=%7B6621b54b-4739-4827-859a-eebd9229657c%7D

- The **"Send Alert" form** for a document or item: \<site URL\>/_layouts/15/SubNew.aspx?List=\<List ID\>&ID=[ID]

The links described above work fine when users upload files to a library and do not change the file names.

When a new document is created in SharePoint, there will probably be a problem with links that include the dynamic field "File name with extension":

1. A user creates a document that automatically gets the name Document1.docx.

2. The flow sends an e-mail with a link to the document.

3. The user changes the file name into something more descriptive.

4. A flow cannot change file names in the already sent e-mails, so the link will not work.

Adding a delay to the flow will solve that problem in most cases, *refer to* 5.3.3, Delay a flow.

Demo:

https://kalmstrom.com/Tips/SharePoint-Flows/Flow-E-mail-Links.htm

16 ROLL BACK COLUMN CHANGES

If you want to make sure that a SharePoint column value stays the same, you can add a flow that reacts to changes. This example flow reacts by rolling back any changes of the value in a "Department Name" column to the original one.

As we are using a flow, the rollback will work even if you are using the column value in Microsoft Access, in a mobile or elsewhere.

16.1 PREREQUISITES

A SharePoint *Departments* list with these columns:

- The 'Title' column has been renamed to "Department Name".

- A Single line of text column, "Original Department Name". This column should be hidden from the view when the flow has been finalized.

I recommend that you enable Version history in the list, so that you can see if any changes have been made. Even if they are rolled back by the flow, they will still be visible in the Version history.

16.2 THEORY

We actually only need the flow to run when the value of the "Department Name" column has been modified, but Microsoft Flow does not have a separate trigger for when an item or a specific field has been modified. Instead, we must use the "created or modified" trigger, which runs the flow both on new items and with every change.

The "Department Name" value of the new item is the original one that must be kept. Therefore, we must find a way to let the flow understand what triggered the flow. Was it a creation of a new item or a modification of an existing item?

To achive that distinction in the flow, we will use the fact that all SharePoint columns have a "null" value from start, before another value has been added.

16.3 STEPS

As the trigger has two parameters, "created" and "modified", we must first find out which parameter has actually triggered the flow. If the item has been "created" it is new, and the "Original Department Name" column should not have been filled out, as it is hidden from users.

This distinction is made in the first condition, and if this condition is true – and the item is new – its "Department Name" value will be saved in the "Original Department Name" column.

If the condition is false – and the item is not new – the flow must check if the "Department Name" value is the same as the original or not. If the value is different, the flow must react and in this case roll back the value to the original one.

1. Create a blank flow and use the trigger 'SharePoint - when an item is created or modified' for the *Departments* list.

2. Add a condition to check which one of the two trigger parameters are valid in this case – "created" or "modified":

   a. The dynamic content 'Original Department Name'

   b. is equal to

   c. the function 'null'. Under Expressions, start writing "null" and select it when it is shown in the dropdown.

3. If the condition is true (= the item is new), add the action 'SharePoint – update item' for the *Departments* list:

   a. At Id, add the dynamic content 'ID' for the new item.

   b. At 'Department Name' add the dynamic content 'Department Name' for the new item.

   c. At 'Original Department Name' add the dynamic content 'Department Name'.

4. If the condition is false (= the item has been modified), add another condition to check the value of the "Department Name" column:

   a. The dynamic content 'Original Department Name'

   b. is *not* equal to

c. the dynamic content 'Department Name'.

5. If the second condition is true (= the values are not the same), add the action 'SharePoint – update item' for the *Departments* list:

    a. At Id, add the dynamic content 'ID' for the item.

    b. At 'Department Name' add the dynamic content 'Original Department Name' for the item.

6. Save and test the flow.

Demo:

https://www.kalmstrom.com/Tips/SharePoint-Flows/Flow-Rollback.htm

17 SET TASK ASSIGNEE DEPENDING ON CATEGORY

When people fill out an order or a support or issue tracking ticket in a SharePoint list or form, they seldom know the name of the person who will take care of their request. That value has to be set manually – or by a flow.

What people know, or can figure out, is what category their order or issue belongs to, and from that information we can let a flow assign the default responsible for each item. The default responsible can either manage the request (which should be happening most often) or assign the ticket to someone else.

This example flow runs when a new task has been created in a *Tickets* list. It reads the value of the "Ticket Category" column in the new item and picks the default assignee for that category from a settings list.

If a person needs to be replaced as default assignee, just edit the settings list and set a new default assignee. The flow will not be affected. It will continue to run as before and just show the new person as responsible for that category in the tickets.

Connector: SharePoint

17.1 PREREQUISITES:

- A *Tickets* list built on the Tasks template with a custom Choice column for "Ticket Category". This column is mandatory to fill out.

  The 'Assigned To', column has a description that tells that it will be filled out by a flow. Multiple selections are not allowed in 'Assigned To'.

  Users fill out the *Tickets* list, or a custom form connected to that list, with a task name and a description and select ticket category from a dropdown.

- A custom *Ticket Rules* list where the 'Title' column name has been changed into "Comment". This column does not require a value.

  The *Ticket Rules* list also has these columns:

  o A Choice column for "Ticket Category".

  o A Person or Group column, "Default Assignee".

Both lists should have the same choice options in the "Ticket Category" column, so it is best to create a site column that you can re-use, but two list columns will also work.

The flow will work even if you don't enter a default assignee for all ticket categories.

17.2 THEORY

In this flow we use a dynamic content contained in a string. The beginning and end of a string should be marked with apostrophes, like this: 'DC' where DC is the dynamic content.

We also use "eq" in a query. This means "equals" and is often used in queries and strings. You will see it in several places in later example flows.

"Claims" is the Active Directory Security object that represents a user. This flow sets a value for 'Assigned To' in a *Tickets* list, so when we use dynamic content 'Default Assignee Claims' from the *Ticket Rules* list for the 'Assign To Claims' field, the two lists become connected.

17.3 STEPS

1. Create a blank flow and use the trigger 'SharePoint - when an item is created' for the *Tickets* list.

2. Add the action 'SharePoint - Get items' for the *Ticket Rules* list. (Only one item will be fetched, but if we use 'get item' we need to know the item ID.)

3. At 'Filter Query' under advanced options, enter the internal name "TicketCategory" + eq + a string with the dynamic content 'Ticket Category Value' for the current item.

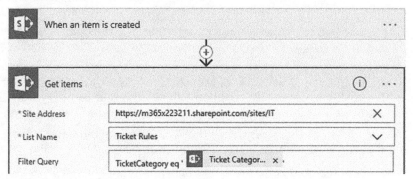

4. Add an 'Apply to each' action and set the output value to the dynamic content 'value'.

5. Add the action 'SharePoint - Update item' for the *Tickets* list to the 'Apply to each' action.

   a. At 'Id', add the dynamic content 'ID' from 'When an item is created'.

   b. At 'Task Name', add the dynamic content 'Task Name' from 'When an item is created'.

c. Remove any default values. (If you don't do that, the flow will overwrite any values that users enter with the default ones.)

d. At 'Assigned To Claims', add the dynamic content 'Default Assignee Claims' from the 'Get items' action as a custom value.

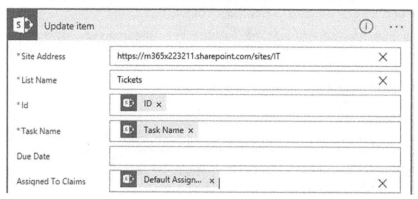

6. Save the flow and test it by creating a new item in the *Tickets* list. When you open it again, the default assignee should have been filled out automatically.

Demo:

https://www.kalmstrom.com/Tips/SharePoint-Flows/Flow-Ticket-Category-Assigned.htm

18 MERGE ORDERS INTO A TASKS LIST

Most companies have a department that handles a lot of different tasks for the rest of the organization. Here we are using this common scenario to show how you can re-use a flow by first exporting it and then importing it and create a new flow from it.

My imaginary department manages delivery of computers, flowers and tables. As there are three different forms, it is easy to order. Each order form only contains the columns needed for a special kind of item.

We also imagine that the same people will fulfill all the orders, no matter what has been ordered. These people don't want to check orders in three lists.

Instead, the handlers want all data that users enter in the order forms to be transferred to one *Tasks* list. This can be done with flows, one for each order list, that fetch data from the order lists and create new items in the *Tasks* list.

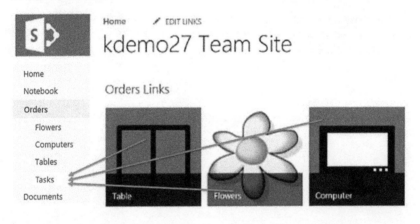

Instead of creating three flows, we will only create the flow for Computers from scratch. Then we will export the Computers flow, import it twice as new flows and change the applicable details to get it to work with Flowers and Tables.

Connector: SharePoint

18.1 PREREQUISITES

- A *Tasks* SharePoint list built on the Tasks template.

- Three SharePoint order forms/lists, *Computers*, *Flowers* and *Tables*.

- *Computers* and *Tables* are used for orders within the company, and the 'Title' columns in those lists are renamed to 'Comment' and is not mandatory.

- The flower orders are mostly intended for customers, and its 'Title' column is renamed 'Phone number'.
- The lists also have the following columns, all mandatory:
  - *Computers*: a Choice column, "Type of Computer" and a Person or Group column, "User".
  - *Flowers*: a Choice column, "Type of Bouquet" and a Single line of text column, "Recipient". (A Person or Group column cannot be used for people outside the tenant.)
  - *Tables*: a Choice column, "Type of Table", and a Single line of text column, "House", with the description text "Please specify where the table should be placed".

18.2 THEORY

In this flow we will make practical use of the Flow export/import feature. To understand the flow, you must also know that there is a list behind each SharePoint form.

I wanted to show the export/import feature, which is most often used to share flows. To not complicate the demo that way, I exported and imported my own flows, but for this flow I could also have used the Save as feature, *refer to* 6.4, Start from an Existing Flow.

18.2.1 *SharePoint*

A SharePoint form is always connected to a list, and in this flow we are using the lists behind three SharePoint forms. The lists have the same names as the forms. When someone fills out one of the forms, a new item is created in the corresponding list. The column values in those list items will be used in the flow.

18.2.2 *Flow*

Refer to 7.2, Export and Import Flows, for details on how to export and import flows.

18.3 STEPS

1. Create the flow from blank and select the trigger 'SharePoint – When an item is created' for the *Computers* list.
2. Add the action 'SharePoint – Create item' for the *Tasks* list.
3. The *Tasks* columns will be loaded to the flow, so that you can add text and dynamic content to applicable columns. Columns that should be filled out by the person who handles the order are left empty here. (That person probably assigns the task to someone,

sets a priority and a due date and eventually marks the task as completed when the order is fulfilled.)

a. Build the Title with hardcoded text and dynamic content from the item that was created in the *Computers* list, like this: New + 'Type of computer' + for + 'User DisplayName'.

b. Build the description in the same way. Use HTML so that you get the information nicely arranged.

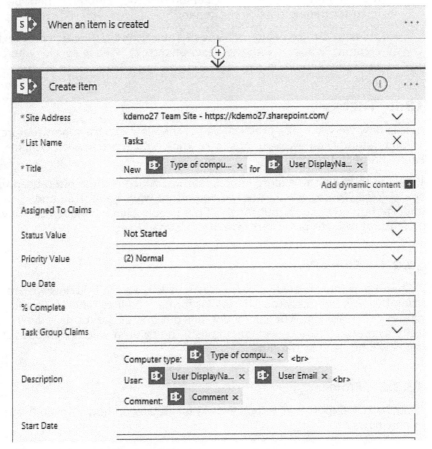

4. Save the flow and rename it "Computer orders".

5. Test the flow by performing the trigger action: Fill out the *Computers* form and make sure that a new task is created in the *Tasks* list and that it contains the information specified in step 3.

6. Export the Computer orders flow as a .zip package and then import it to the Flow site as a new flow (or Save the flow as). Call the new flow "Flower orders".

7. Edit the flow and change the name of the trigger list to *Flowers*. Also change the text and dynamic content in the *Tasks* list (added in step 3) to suit flower orders.

8. Test the Flower orders flow by filling out the *Flowers* form.

9. Import the Computer orders flow to the Flow site as a new flow again (or use 'Save as'). Call the new flow "Table orders".

10. Edit the flow and change the name of the trigger list to *Tables*. Also change the text and dynamic content in the *Tasks* list (added in step 3) to suit table orders.

11. Test the Table orders flow.

Similar flows can be used whenever people input data in an online form. It can be requests for a quote or survey results, and the services might be Excel Surveys or Microsoft Forms. Flow also supports multiple third party forms solutions that give input from users.

In the next chapters, we will give two other examples on how to let a flow add information to a SharePoint list: one flow that gets data from a Forms survey and one that gets data from Dropbox.

Demo:

https://www.kalmstrom.com/Tips/SharePoint-Flows/Flow-Orders-To-Tasks.htm

19 Copy Survey Responses from Forms

Microsoft Forms is an online survey creator included in most Office 365 subscriptions. It helps you create surveys, quizzes, polls and other forms. To reach respondents, you can either embed the form in a web page or send a link to it.

The answers can be seen in Forms, and you can also open the result in Excel directly from the Forms site. It is however often convenient to work with respondent data in SharePoint, and in this example flow we direct the responses to two different SharePoint lists.

Connector: Microsoft Forms, SharePoint

19.1 Prerequisites:

- A Forms survey, *Customer Survey*, that is answered by people outside the company. (They have no access to the Office 365 tenant.) The survey contains the questions "Name", "Email" and "Do you want to receive a newsletter?". (I show how to create such a flow in the demo article I link to at the end of this chapter.)

- A SharePoint *Leads* list for survey responses. A new item is created for each respondent, and that person's name is added to the 'Title' field. His/her responses to all questions except the newsletter question are entered in the 'Description' field.

- A SharePoint *Newsletter* list for all respondents who answer yes to the question about newsletter. The name of the respondent is placed in the 'Title', and there is a single line of text column for the respondent's e-mail address.

I recommend a tasks or issue tracking list for *Leads* and a custom list for *Newsletters*.

19.2 Theory

You should be logged in to Office 365 as the same user when you create the form and the flow. Then you will be able to pick the form you want to get data from when you create the flow.

In this flow we can directly select an action that gets Form details, 'Forms - Get response details', without having to first add a loop action for all the survey responses. That step is included in the Forms action and when you create the flow you can see that it is added automatically.

When you have connected the flow to the survey, the survey questions come up as dynamic content in the flow. What you actually get is of course not the questions but the *answers* to those questions.

19.3 STEPS

I recommend that you save and test the flow after step 4, when you have added responses to the *Leads* list, before you continue with the *Newsletter* list. That way it is easier to correct mistakes, if any.

1. Create a blank flow and use the trigger 'Microsoft Forms - When a new response is submitted' for the *Customer Survey* form.

2. Add the action 'Forms - Get response details' for the *Customer Survey* form. Add the dynamic content 'Response Id'. (Click on 'More' if you cannot see it.)

3. Now an 'apply to each' action will be created automatically. It loops the dynamic content 'List of response notifications' and gets the details.

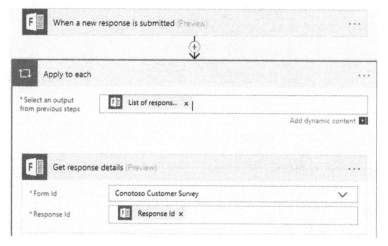

4. Add the action 'SharePoint – Create item' for the *Leads* list.

   a. In the 'Title' field, add some general text, like "New lead", and the dynamic content 'Name' from the survey.

   b. In the 'Description' field, add dynamic content for responses to all survey questions except "Do you want to receive a newsletter?". Also add suitable text before the dynamic content, so that you recognize which question each response belongs to.

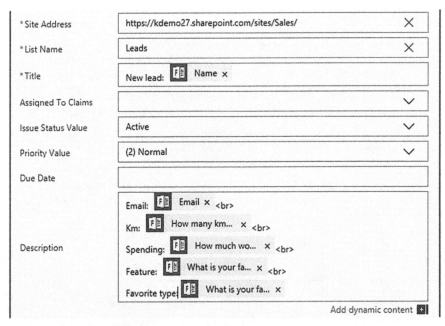

5. Save and test the flow.

6. Add a condition: if the dynamic content 'Do you want to receive a newsletter?' is equal to 'Yes'.

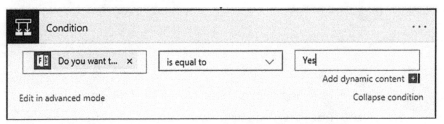

7. If the condition is true, add the action 'SharePoint – Create item' for the *Newsletter* list.

8. Add the dynamic content 'Name' from the survey at 'Title' and the dynamic content 'Email' from the survey at 'Email address'.

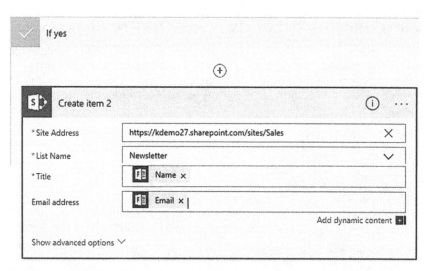

9. Save and test the flow.

A more advanced flow can send the responses to different columns in the *Leads* list, instead of adding them all to the description field, but the process for the flow is the same.

Demo:

https://www.kalmstrom.com/Tips/SharePoint-Flows/Flow-Forms-to-SharePoint.htm

20 COPY REQUESTED DROPBOX FILES TO SHAREPOINT

Sometimes you need to get files from people outside the organization into a SharePoint library, but you don't want to create SharePoint accounts for them. Of course, you can receive files by e-mail and upload them to SharePoint yourself, but that is troublesome when there are many files.

Using a cloud service for document sharing will not burden your mailbox, but it will give the same trouble to get the files to SharePoint, and on top of that it will require a login.

A better way is to use a Dropbox "Requested files" folder, and combine it with a flow and a custom library template. A flow can send info from the files in the Dropbox folder into new files in a SharePoint library. With this method, the process will be automatic, and no login will be required.

My example uses quotations from restaurants, for a staff party. Such information is not sensitive, so I can use the Dropbox folder without taking risks if the link is shared. The quotation form should be restricted, so that users only can fill out the form and not modify the template.

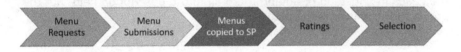

20.1 PREREQUISITES

- A Word template with a form to fill out. One of the form fields is "Cost per guest". Word files with such forms are sent to restaurant owners as e-mail attachments. Each e-mail contains a link to a "Requested files" folder in Dropbox.

- A Dropbox "Requested files" folder. Restaurant owners fill out the forms and upload them to the Dropbox "Requested files" folder.

- A SharePoint *Kick Off Menus* library with two custom columns: a "Cost per guest" column and a "Rating" column. Both these columns are shown in the default view. A flow copies the information in each filled out Word form to corresponding new files in the SharePoint library, where the suggestions can be seen and rated.

The creation of a Dropbox "Requested files" folder is out of scope for this book, just as the custom SharePoint library columns and the custom Word form that should be used as a library template. You should have some prior knowledge about all that, to try this solution, but I describe the steps in detail in the Tips article I have linked to after the Steps. Here I will concentrate on the flow.

20.2 THEORY

Dropbox is a third party file hosting service. When the information uploaded to Dropbox is contained in document fields that correspond to SharePoint library columns, a flow can copy field content from Dropbox files into new files in the SharePoint library.

"Requested files" folders in Dropbox do not require log in from people who have a link to the folder.

20.3 STEPS

1. On the Flow site home page, click on 'Connectors' in the left pane and find Dropbox.

2. Select the template 'When a file is created'.

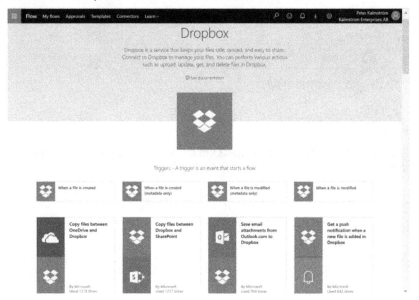

3. Click on the picker to the right in the folder box and select a Dropbox folder for file requests.

4. Add the action 'SharePoint – Create file' for the *Kick Off Menus* library. This action will create a file in SharePoint based on the content in each uploaded Dropbox file.

a. Insert the dynamic Dropbox content 'File name' in the field 'File name'.

b. Insert the dynamic Dropbox content 'File content' in the field 'File content'.

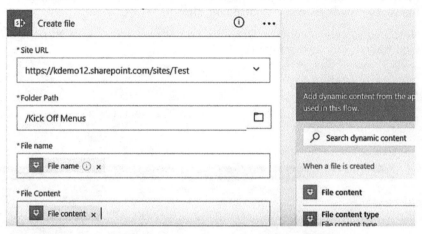

5. Save and test the flow.

Demo:

http://www.kalmstrom.com/Tips/Office-365-Course/Flow-Dropbox-SharePoint.htm

21   NEW EMPLOYEE TASKS

When new people join an organization, there are certain things that always have to be done. The new employees will for example need some equipment, and the people responsible for arranging that must be informed.

In this example, we will build two different flows that create SharePoint tasks with information about new staff and what equipment is needed.

Connector: SharePoint

21.1   NEW EMPLOYEE *TASKS* WITHOUT A SETTINGS LIST

In this flow, each piece of equipment is written into the flow. This means that the flow must be changed every time there is a change in the equipment. If you don't do that, the flow will stop working. Also *refer to* 5.4, Hard-coded Text.

21.1.1   *Prerequisites*

For this example flow, we need two SharePoint lists (on the same or different sites).

- An *Employees* list with staff information. New people are added as new items in the list when they are hired.

  The list contains three columns: "First name", "Last name" and a choice column, "Position". The choices are "Finance", "Management" and "Production".

- A *Workflow Tasks* list. The flow creates tasks in this list. Each task contains information on one equipment item and the name of the new employee who needs it. The equipment depends on which position the new employee is placed in.

  o   Finance: a computer and a desk

  o   Management: a computer, a Visa card and an office

  o   Production: a tablet and protection gear

By using one task per equipment item, we can give different people or groups the responsibility for each item needed by the new employee.

21.1.2   *Theory*

When you use a SharePoint choice column in a flow, you must make sure to get the value of that column. For example, in this flow you can choose between the dynamic contents 'Position', which only gives you the choice number, and 'Position value'.

This flow is not difficult to understand, but it takes time to build. When this is written, it is not possible to copy and paste actions in Flow, so you have to create actions for each task separately. In this case, it means that you have to create seven different actions and for each action specify the same site URL and tasks list name.

21.1.3 Steps

We will create three conditions, one for each position value, and then we create one task for each equipment item needed by staff in that position:

- If Management is true, create tasks for computer, Visa and office.
- If Finance is true, create tasks for computer and desk.
- If Production is true, create tasks for tablet and protection gear.

1. Create a blank flow and use the trigger 'SharePoint - When an item is created' for the *Employees* list.

2. Add a condition for the dynamic content 'Position value' in the *Employees* list: If the Position value is equal to Management.

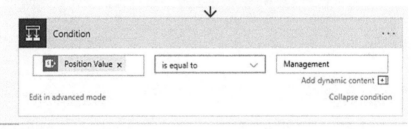

   a. 'If yes':

   i. Add the action 'SharePoint - Create item' for the Workflow Tasks list. At 'Task Name' under the advanced options, add the text "Computer for" + the dynamic contents for 'First Name' and 'Last Name'.

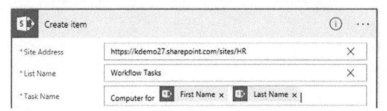

   ii. Add a new action, 'SharePoint - create item' for the Workflow Tasks list. At 'Task Name', add the text "Visa for" + the dynamic contents for 'First Name' and 'Last Name'.

iii. Add a new action, 'SharePoint - create item' for the *Workflow Tasks* list. At 'Task Name', add the text "Office for" + the dynamic contents for 'First Name' and 'Last Name'.

b. 'If no', add a condition: if the dynamic content 'Position value' is equal to Finance.

    i. 'If yes', add two new actions, 'SharePoint - Create item' for the *Workflow Tasks* list, one for the computer and one for the desk.

    ii. 'If no', the third Position value, "Production", must be true. Add two new actions, 'SharePoint - Create item' for the *Workflow Tasks* list, one for the tablet and one for the protection gear.

3. Save and test the flow.

21.2 NEW EMPLOYEE TASKS WITH A SETTINGS LIST

To further automate and enhance the process, I recommend that you let the flow fetch the equipment items from a *Hiring Settings* list instead of hard-coding them. With such a list, you avoid changes in the flow each time anything including equipment is changed, and you can also easily set and change the responsible for each item. Even if column values are changed, the flow will continue to work as before.

When you use a settings list, the flow may be more complicated to understand, but it is quicker to create. As users can make value changes in the *Hiring Settings* list without disturbing the flow, this flow is much more convenient to use in the long run.

21.2.1 Prerequisites

For this flow, we need the same two SharePoint lists as in the previous flow, the *Employees* list and the *Workflow Tasks* list. We are also using the same pieces of equipment as in the previous flow.

New for this flow is that we also use a *Hiring Settings* list with information about what equipment is needed and who is responsible for the task. Rename the 'Title' column to "What To Do?" and enter equipment values in that column. (In the flow dynamic content, this column will still be shown as 'Title'.)

To Do ∨	Position ∨	Assigned To ∨
Computer	Finance	Peter Kalmström
Computer	Management	Peter Kalmström
Tablet	Production	Dipti Francis
Office	Management	Vipul Dindulkar
Protection gear	Production	Jitu Patidar
Desk	Finance	Rituka Rimza
Visa	Management	Jayant Rimza

The *Hiring Settings* list has a Choice column for "Position", with the same values as in the *Employees* list: "Finance", "Management" and "Production".

The *Hiring Settings* list also has a Person or Group column that shows who is responsible for arranging each piece of equipment.

21.2.2   Theory

As we want a new item to be created for each piece of equipment, we must first filter out the equipment items that are needed for the "Position" value in the new item. Therefore, we use a Filter Query for the "Get items" action.

The query reads the position value in the new item that triggered the flow and gives all items in the *Hiring Settings* list that has this position value. So, if the position value is for example "Finance", two items will be found: one for the computer and one for the desk.

Then we use an 'Apply to each' action to loop through the found items and create a new item in the *Workflow Tasks* list for each one of them. In that process, the flow also fetches the assigned person or group from the *Hiring Settings* list and adds that to the new item.

21.2.3   Steps

1. Create a blank flow and use the trigger 'SharePoint - When an item is created' for the *Employees* list.

2. Add an action: 'SharePoint - Get items' for the *Hiring Settings* list.

3. At 'Filter Query' under advanced options, filter the Position value so that it equals the dynamic content 'Position value'. Add apostrophes around the dynamic content in the field to make it a string.

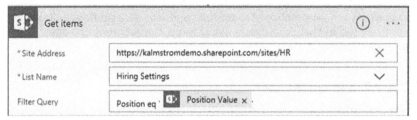

4. Add an action: 'Apply to each'. Select the dynamic content 'value' from the 'Get items' action as output.

5. Add an action for the 'Apply to each': 'SharePoint - Create item', to create a task in the *Workflow Tasks* list.

   a. At 'Task Name' write some general text and add dynamic content from the trigger for 'First name', 'Last name' and 'Title' (Title is renamed in the list and contains the equipment items).

   b. At 'Assigned To Claims', add the dynamic content 'Assigned Claims' from the 'Get items' action.

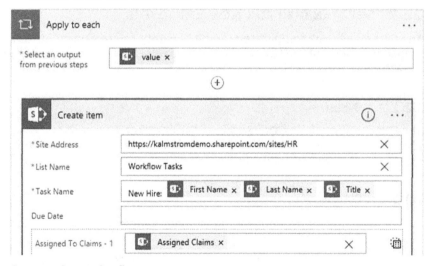

6. Save and test the flow.

Demo:

https://www.kalmstrom.com/Tips/SharePoint-Flows/Flow-Employment-Process.htm

22 KEEP TWO LISTS IN SYNC

In this chapter we will look at two example flows that both work on the same lists. The first flow will update an *Employees* list with the manager name when a new employee is added, and the second flow will update all employees in the *Employees* list when a department changes manager.

22.1 PREREQUISITES

These example flows use the same two custom lists:

- A *Departments* list where the Title column is renamed into "Department Name". This list also has a Person or Group column called "Manager".

- An *Employees* list with a lookup column for "Department" that picks values to choose among from the "Department Name" column in the *Departments* list.

The *Employees* list also has a Person or Group "Manager" column. Its description field explains that the value will be set by a flow.

22.2 SET MANAGER FOR NEW EMPLOYEES

The first flow is not complicated, and it is surely convenient to have the manager added automatically when you have selected a new employee's department!

22.2.1 Theory

The 'Title' column in the Departments list has been renamed to "Department Name', but as the flow needs the internal name in the Filter Query to get items, we still use 'Title' here.

22.2.2 Steps

1. Create a blank flow and use the trigger 'SharePoint - when an item is created' for the *Employees* list.

2. Add the action 'SharePoint - Get items' for the "Departments" list.

3. At 'Filter Query' under advanced options, enter Title + eq + a string with the dynamic content 'Department Value' for the created item.

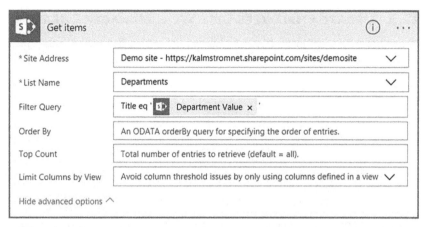

4. Add an 'apply to each' action and set the output value to the dynamic content 'value' from the 'Get items' action.

5. Add the action 'SharePoint - Update item' for the *Employees* list to the Apply to each action.

   a. At 'Id', add the dynamic content 'ID' from the trigger.

   b. At 'Title', add the dynamic content 'Title' from the trigger.

   c. Remove any default values. Otherwise the flow will overwrite any values set in an *Employees* list item with the default values.

   d. At 'Manager Claims', add the dynamic content 'Manager Claims' from the 'Get items' action as a custom value.

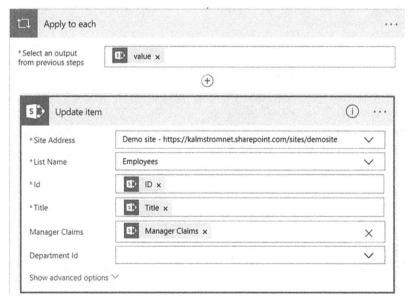

6. Save and test the flow.

22.3 Update Employees List With Manager Changes

The second flow updates the *Employees* list when there is a manager change in the *Departments* list.

22.3.1 Theory

A Lookup column fetches its data from another list, but values in a Person or Group column cannot be picked by a lookup column. Instead we can let a flow fetch the value in the Person or Group column.

One benefit of having the managers in a Person or Group column, is that each manager can filter employees by "My Team" to show only people in that manager's department in a view filtered by [Me].

"Claims" is the Active Directory Security object that represents a user, and in this flow we use the 'Manager Claims' parameter.

22.3.2 Steps

1. Create a blank flow and use the trigger 'SharePoint - when an item is created or modified' for the *Departments* list.

2. Add the action 'SharePoint – Get items' for the *Employees* list, to get all the employees in the department of the created or modified item.

3. At 'Filter Query' under Advanced options, enter "Department + eq + the dynamic content for 'ID' in a string. (Add apostrophes around ID to make it a string.)

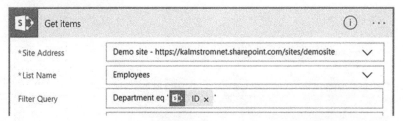

4. Add an Apply to each action and enter the output as the dynamic content for 'value' from the 'Get items' action.

5. Add the action 'SharePoint – Update item' for the *Employees* list.

   a. The 'Id' is the dynamic content for the ID from 'Get items'.

   b. The mandatory 'Title' is the dynamic content 'Title' from 'Get items'.

   c. At 'Manager Claims' choose to enter a custom value and select the dynamic content 'Manager Claims' from the trigger action.

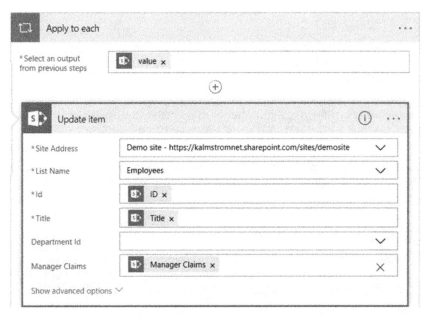

6. Save and test the flow.

23 REMINDERS

Flows can be used for different kinds of reminders. Automatic reminder e-mails are good to have when a contract has to be re-negotiated, an important event must be remembered or a subscription should be renewed.

I will give two different examples on how reminder flows can be created. The first flow runs every day, and the second flow runs seven days before a specific date.

Both these flows use the trigger 'Schedule – Recurrence', so you can start them manually from the 'My flows' page, *refer to* 5.2.3, Recurrence.

23.1 EVENT REMINDER

The flow outlined below sends e-mail reminders of events that are created in a SharePoint calendar called *Meetings*. The reminder is sent at 07.00 in the morning on the same day as the event.

Connectors: Office 365 Outlook, Schedule, SharePoint

23.1.1 *Prerequisites*

A SharePoint calendar called *Meetings*.

23.1.2 *Theory*

When you use the action 'Get items' you will get all items. To discern specific items, in this case today's items, we will use the action `Apply to each' in this flow. The 'Apply to each' action will loop through all items in the calendar list.

A condition will then decide which items should be used in the flow, and I will give the formula for that condition in step 4.a below.

23.1.3 *Steps*

In this flow, a 'Recurrence' trigger will initiate and repeat the process of sending a reminder at a given time.

1. Create a blank flow with the trigger 'Schedule – Recurrence' and set the frequency and time for when it should run.

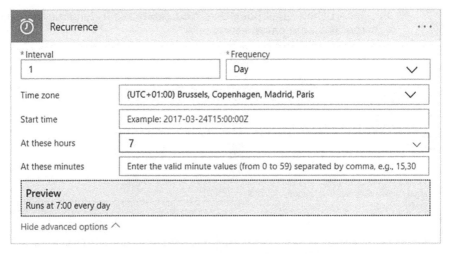

2. Add the action 'SharePoint – Get items' for the calendar list *Meetings*.

3. Add an 'Apply to each' action and insert the dynamic content 'value' from the 'Get items' action as output.

4. Add an action for the 'Apply to each' and select 'Condition'.

   a. Click on 'Edit in advanced mode' and enter the condition: @equals(substring(item()?['EventDate'], 0, 10),utcnow('yyyy-MM-dd')). This will fill out the condition fields in basic mode.

   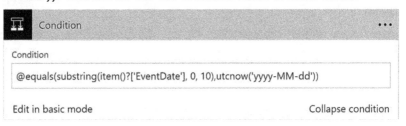

   b. Here 'item()' refers to the current item of the list and '['EventDate']' is the column that should be checked. The condition will be true for "Today's Date". *Refer to* https://powerusers.microsoft.com/t5/Building-Flows/Use-Today-date-parameter/td-p/1432, if you want to learn more about the creation of this formula.

   c. 'If yes', add the action 'Office 365 Outlook - Send an email'.

      i. In the 'To' field, enter the users who should have reminder e-mails when the condition is true.

      ii. For the e-mail subject, enter "Meeting reminder" or other general text and the dynamic content 'Title' from the 'Get items' action.

iii. Insert the e-mail body text. You can make it dynamic by using the available parameters.

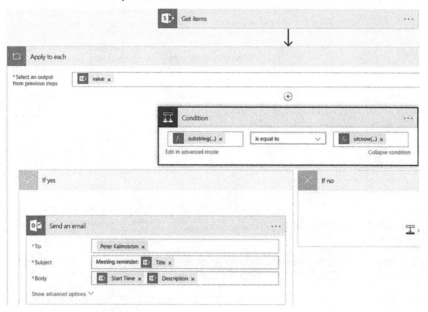

5. Save and test the flow.

Demo:

http://www.kalmstrom.com/Tips/Office-365-Course/Reminder-Through-Microsoft-Flow.htm

23.2 CONTRACT REVIEW REMINDER

It is a good idea to store company contracts in a SharePoint library, and if you do that you can set a flow to send a reminder to the person who is responsible for either renewing or cancelling each contract when it expires.

In this flow we will use an expression that sets the reminder date to seven days before the contract's expiry date.

Connectors: Office 365 Outlook, Schedule, SharePoint

23.2.1 Prerequisites

A *Contracts* library with a Person or Group column called "Responsible Counsel" and a Date and Time column called "Renewal or Expiry Date".

As the internal name must be used for the Expiry date column in the query formula, I recommend that you use CamelCase naming for this column, *refer to* 2.3 CamelCase Naming. If you haven't done that, there are URL decoder sites online that can help you get the internal name from a column name.

23.2.2   Theory

When you use a list with a 'Person or Group' column in a flow, the flow automatically gets a number of properties from the user object, such as department and e-mail address. That information can of course be very useful in the flow, and here we use it to have the e-mail address of the responsible counsel, in step 5 of the flow. That person needs to have an account in the tenant. Otherwise you cannot use the 'Person or Group' column.

All document libraries are built on top of the content type Document, which has a Name property used for storing the name of the file. This property is used in the e-mail part of the flow at point 8.

In this example flow we will use a 'Get items' action, just like in the earlier reminder flow. We will however discern the items to be used with a filter query instead of using a condition. I give the formula for the query that filters out the contracts that expire 7 days after today in the flow step 3.

23.2.3   Steps

1. Create the flow from blank and use the trigger 'Schedule – Recurrence'.

2. Set the 'interval' to '1' and the 'Frequency' to 'Day'. Set your preferred time under advanced options.

3. Add the action 'SharePoint - Get items' for the *Contracts* library.

    a. At 'Filter Query', enter the internal name for the "Renewal or Expiry Date" column + eq. Add an apostrophe (') to start building a string. Then build an expression for the rest of the field:

        i.   In the function field, start writing "format" and then select 'formatDateTime'.

        ii. Add a parenthesis for input and start writing "add" inside it. Select 'addDays'.

        iii. Add another parenthesis and start writing "utc" inside it. Select 'utcNow'. That will also add a new parenthesis to the function.

        iv. After the new parenthesis, enter a comma (,) and 7 (for seven days).

v. Before the last parenthesis, add a comma and a string. Enter the date format, by ISO standard yyyy-MM-dd, in the string.

vi. You should now have this expression: FormatDateTime(addDays(utcNow(),7),'yyy-MM-dd'). That filters out the contracts that expire 7 days after today, which was our business rule for when reminders are to be sent out.

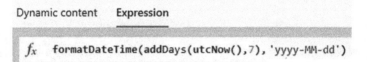

Dynamic content **Expression**

f_x formatDateTime(addDays(utcNow(),7), 'yyyy-MM-dd')

b. Place the cursor after the start of string apostrophe in the 'Filter Query' field and click OK to the expression.

c. Add an end of string apostrophe in the 'Filter Query' field.

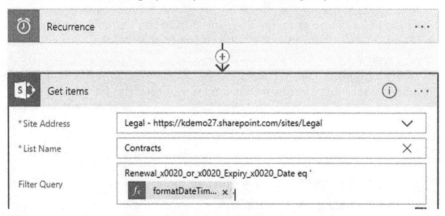

4. Add an 'Apply to each' action and use the dynamic content 'value' from the 'Get items' action as output.

5. Add the action 'Office 365 Outlook - Send an email'.

a. In the 'To' field, enter the dynamic content 'ResponsibleCounselE-mail' from the 'Get items' action.

b. For the e-mail subject, type some general text and add the name of the contract with the dynamic content 'Name' from the 'Get items' action.

c. Insert a link in the 'Body' field:

i. Under advanced options, set 'Is HTML' to Yes.

ii. Enter <a href="[the dynamic content 'Link to Item']">Some general text</a>.

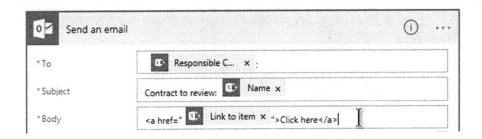

Demo:

https://www.kalmstrom.com/Tips/SharePoint-Flows/Flow-Contract-Reminder.htm

24 SEND E-MAILS WITH ATTACHMENTS FROM SHARED MAILBOX

This example flow takes information from a SharePoint list and adds it to an outgoing e-mail that is sent from a shared mailbox. Using a flow and a SharePoint list can sometimes be better than sending from the shared mailbox directly.

When sending e-mails to people outside the organization, such as customers or suppliers, it can be valuable that the flow handles attachments as well, so I have included attachments in the flow. That has made it a bit more complicated – but also more interesting, I hope!

Connectors: Office 365 Outlook, SharePoint

24.1 PREREQUISITES

- A SharePoint list, *Outgoing Email* where attachments are enabled (which is default). The 'Title' column is renamed to "Subject", and there is a multiple lines of text column called "Body" and a single line of text column called "To".

- An Exchange shared mailbox.

24.2 THEORY

In some cases, it is better to let users add e-mail details to a SharePoint list instead of sending the information directly from a shared mailbox. You will have a better control of what is sent, and the data in the SharePoint list can be sorted, filtered, searched and displayed in different views.

Furthermore, you don't have to give a lot of people access to the shared mailbox. They only need permission to create items in the SharePoint list.

The e-mails will be sent with the shared mailbox account, for example support@company.com, as the sender. You should use that shared mailbox account when you create the flow.

The attachments will be contained in an array variable.

24.3 STEPS

If you don't want to give users a possibility to send attachments, you can skip steps 2-6 below and just use the trigger and the send e-mail action.

1. Create the flow from blank and use the trigger 'SharePoint - When an item is created' for the *Outgoing Email* list.

2. Add an action to contain the attachments: 'Variables – initialize variable'. Give it a name and select the type 'Array'.

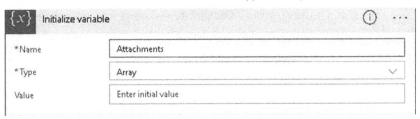

3. Add an action to get the attachments from the list item: 'SharePoint - Get attachments' for the *Outgoing Email* list.

4. At 'Id' add the dynamic content 'ID' for the trigger item.

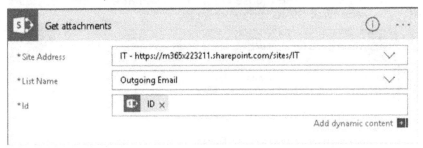

5. Add an 'Apply to each' action to loop through the attachments. Use the dynamic content 'Body' from the 'Get attachments' action as output.

6. Add the action 'SharePoint - Get attachment content' for the *Outgoing Email* list. At 'Id' and 'File Identifier, add the dynamic contents 'ID' of the created item and 'Id' of the 'Get Attachments' action.

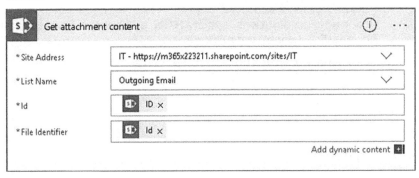

7. Add the 'Get attachment content' action to the array with the action 'Variables - Append to array variable'. Enter the name 'Attachments' and build a JSON object for the 'Value' field:

   a. Start and end the object with curly brackets.

b. Write "Name": and add the dynamic content 'DisplayName' for the attachments. Add a comma after the dynamic content.

c. On the next row, write "ContentBytes": and add an expression:

   i. In the function field, write "body (')".

   ii. Inside the string, add the name of the 'Get attachment content' action. Enter underscore instead of spaces.

   iii. After the end parenthesis, write ".$content".

f_x **body(`'Get_attachment_content'`).$content**

   iv. Make sure the mouse cursor is placed after "ContentBytes": and click OK to the expression.

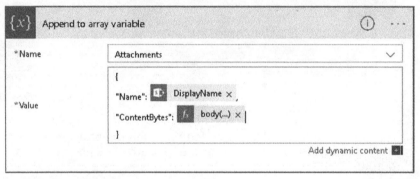

8. Outside the 'Apply to each' loop, add an action: 'Office 365 Outlook - Send an e-mail':

a. Add the dynamic content for the fields 'To', 'Subject' and 'Body' from the trigger item.

b. Under advanced options, specify HTML and set the Importance to Normal (it is Low by default).

c. At Attachments, click on the icon to be able to add an array.

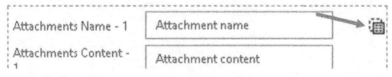

d. Add the dynamic content variable 'Attachments'.

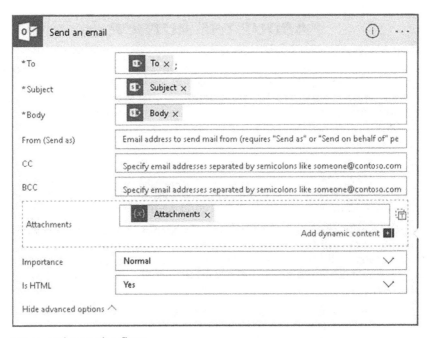

9. Save and test the flow.

Demo:

https://www.kalmstrom.com/Tips/SharePoint-Flows/Flow-E-mails-from-Shared-Mailbox.htm

ABOUT THE AUTHOR

Peter Kalmstrom is the CEO and Systems Designer of the Swedish family business Kalmstrom Enterprises AB, well known for the software brand *kalmstrom.com Business Solutions*. Peter has 19 Microsoft certifications, among them several for SharePoint, and he is a certified Microsoft Trainer.

Peter begun developing his kalmstrom.com products around the turn of the millennium, but for a period of five years, after he had created *Skype for Outlook*, he also worked as a Skype product manager. In 2010 he left Skype, and since then he has been concentrating on his own company and on lecturing on advanced IT courses.

Peter has published four more books, *SharePoint Online from Scratch*, *SharePoint Online Exercises*, *Office 365 from Scratch* and *Excel 2016 from Scratch*. All are sold worldwide via Amazon. He is currently writing a book about SharePoint Designer workflows: *SharePoint Workflows from Scratch*.

As a preparation for lectures and books, Peter has created various video demonstrations, which are available on YouTube and at http://www.kalmstrom.com/Tips.

Peter divides his time between Sweden and Spain. He has three children, and apart from his keen interest in development and new technologies, he likes to sing and act. Peter is also a dedicated vegan and animal rights activist.

INDEX

A

accuracy · 9
action · 26
admin center · 14
apply to each · 29
approval flows · 66
approvals · 20

B

button · 23

C

CamelCase · 11
changes · 10
condition · 28
connector · 17
control action · 28

D

data policies · 15
dedicated account · 10
delay · 30
document titles · 62
dynamic content · 31

E

e-mail report · 83
e-mail sender · 30
environments · 13
export and import · 57
expression · 32

F

Flow mobile app · 72
Flow site · 34
formatting · 88

H

hard-code · 30

L

links in the e-mail body · 90

M

merge orders · 98

N

new employee tasks · 109

P

plans · 13
premium connectors · 13
progress bar · 80

R

recurrence · 25
reminder flows · 118
rename · 43
request sign-off · 20

requested dropbox files · 106
re-use a flow · 98
roll back changes · 92

S

schedule · 21
share · 55
Skype message · 44
speed · 9
storage · 10
survey responses · 102

T

task assignee · 95

team flows · 10
test · 48
totals · 77
tracking · 9
trigger · 23
troubleshoot · 50

V

variable · 21

W

why automate · 9

CPSIA information can be obtained
at www.ICGtesting.com
Printed in the USA
BVHW081926010120
568277BV00001B/110/P